AF394666

HOW TO ENTER THE ART WORLD

AFTER A LATE START, A FIRST CAREER, ILLNESS, RAISING CHILDREN, A CRISIS OF CONFIDENCE, LEAVING IT IN DISGUST...

WRITTEN BY
HETTIE JUDAH

ILLUSTRATED BY
JEMIMA BURRILL

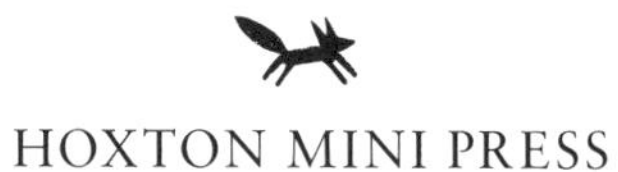

HOXTON MINI PRESS

How to Enter the Art World...
First edition, first printing

Published in 2026 by Hoxton Mini Press, London.
Copyright © Hoxton Mini Press 2026. All rights reserved.
Text © Hettie Judah 2026.
Illustrations © Jemima Burrill 2026.

Text by Hettie Judah
Illustrations by Jemima Burrill
Editing by Florence Ward
Design by Dom Grant
Production control by David Brimble
Proofreading by Dean Drake
Indexing by Emma Caddy

The right of Hettie Judah to be identified as the creator of this Work has been asserted under the Copyright, Designs and Patents Act 1988.

No part of this publication may be reproduced, stored in a retrieval system, or transmitted in any form or by any means, electronic, mechanical, photocopying, recording or otherwise, without the prior written permission of the copyright owner.

A CIP catalogue record for this book is available from the British Library.

ISBN: 978-1-917719-15-5

Printed and bound by OZGraf, Poland

Manufacturer: Hoxton Mini Press, 104 Northside Studios, 16–29 Andrews Road, London E8 4QF, UK. www.hoxtonminipress.com

Represented by: Authorised Rep Compliance Ltd., Ground Floor, 71 Lower Baggot Street, Dublin D02 P593, Ireland. www.arccompliance.com

Hoxton Mini Press is an environmentally conscious publisher, committed to offsetting our carbon footprint. This book is 100 per cent carbon compensated, with offset purchased from Stand For Trees.

Every time you order from our website, we plant a tree: www.hoxtonminipress.com

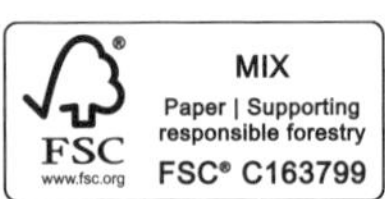

CONTENTS

INTRODUCTION

I will start with a story. It's called *The Successful Artist*. Perhaps you've read it before?

Already tipped as a rising star, the successful artist is accepted onto a noted MA course. The graduate show inspires a feeding frenzy, and the successful artist (who, naturally, favours abstract painting at a heroic scale) is at the heart of it. A mega collector wants every work in the show! But the successful artist is wise. He would not allow one individual such power over his market. He deploys charm and wit to keep the mega collector sweet while dispersing his graduation work. Soon afterwards, he wins an emerging talent award (the first of many) which leads to his nomination for a prestigious residency – three months on a Greek island at a millionaire's private foundation. Thanks to shared interests (Progressive House, the cinema of Paul Verhoeven, Wagyu beef), the two form an intense bond.

On his return, the successful artist signs to a modest but respected gallery in a gritty but up-and-coming part of town. The modest but respected gallery introduces his work to an international audience at modest but respected art fairs. Inclusion in pertinent group shows attracts the attention of a hot-shot young curator who enjoys sounding wise while speaking in front of the successful artist's ever-larger paintings. Hot-shot young curator gives the successful artist a solo exhibition at a regional art centre he has burdened with an ambitious programme. This leads to a larger solo exhibition at another art centre, and then a larger one. Smelling the rapid appreciation of his work, a blue-chip gallery swoops in and lures the successful artist away from the gallery who nurtured his early career. The successful artist speaks of his appreciation for his previous gallery, while recognising they have grown apart. His work enters important collections. By late middle age, the successful artist is feted by the world's greatest museums. He bestrides the world – surgically adjusted spouse on one arm, reputation manager on the other.

The Successful Artist is a work of fiction. Much as tradition dictates that romance novels end in marriage, *The Successful Artist* belongs to a genre of fictions in which all artists' careers take the same shape, moving ever onwards and upwards, building towards a singular vision of success.

These fictions allow speculative collectors to sleep at night, content in the belief that the art they have acquired is accruing value. They allow students to dream that the loans they took to cover years at art school will be paid off. They are fictions that many artists continue to believe right up to the point that real life intervenes and knocks them off track.

This book is your companion for a different route through the art world. Like an old friend, it will be frank, irreverent and occasionally tell you things you don't want to hear. It acknowledges that artists' careers take many shapes – that they go through dips and plateaus, breaks and late starts – and that goals and notions of success may differ.

People take time away from the art world for many reasons. Stepping away can be a terrifying decision, accompanied by a very justified fear that there is no easy route back in. Perhaps you needed stable employment, or to care for your family. Perhaps you suffered years of bad health. Perhaps you lost faith in the art world, or in yourself. Maybe you felt burnt out from the pressure to hustle and promote yourself. This book is for you, and everyone who didn't consider art until later in life because some mealy-mouthed killjoy (or a beloved parent) once said it was not for them.

Since the early 1990s, I have been involved with the art world as a performer, programmer, curator, critic, editor, art historian, mentor, researcher, educator, organiser and an advocate for the rights of artist parents. *How to Enter the Art World…* has come out of years spent talking to artists in unheated studios, community venues, alternative art schools, local art centres, commercial galleries, national museums and grand academies across Europe and the United States. Often, those in the audience are parents, or have led complicated (a.k.a. human) lives. The title of this book comes from a question I am asked in various configurations everywhere from Bloomington, Indiana, to Gothenburg, Sweden.

Everything you will find in these pages derives from the lived experiences of artists and others in the art world. It's an account of a diverse group of people and the strategies that have worked for them as they've entered or re-entered the art world as adults.

PROLOGUE: REALITY CHECK

Mrs V, my sons' primary school teacher, proudly told me that she started the autumn term as a strict disciplinarian and progressively softened over the course of the school year. This was terrifying for 7-year-olds, but you are a grown-up: you can handle the Mrs V treatment, so I'm starting this book with the bad news.

Art sales only grab the headlines when gobsmacking – the $6.2 million paid for a banana gaffer-taped to the wall (a.k.a. Maurizio Cattelan's *Comedian*, 2019), the $91 million paid for Jeff Koons's *Rabbit* (1986), the $90 million paid for David Hockney's *Portrait of an Artist (Pool with Two Figures)* (1972). These sales give an impression of a world in which artists are raking it in for works that, in some instances, seem little more than glib jokes.

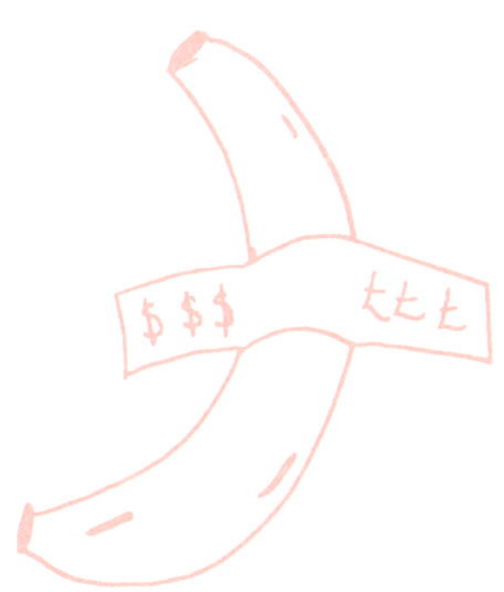

The first thing to note is that the money circulating at these auctions does not go to the artists. Almost all auctions sell works on the secondary market, which means they are being sold by collectors.[1] Strike from your mind the image of Hockney rolling around on a bed of greenbacks after the 2018 sale of *Portrait of an Artist (Pool with Two Figures)*.

Secondly, the wealth visible at auction is far removed from all but a very few artists' experience. Most artists struggle to get by.

Before we get down to business, I want to dive briefly (seven paragraphs max, I promise) into some statistics to build up a realistic picture of artists' working and living conditions. Ok, deep breath…

In 2024, the Artist Earnings Survey – commissioned by the Design & Artists Copyright Society (DACS) and the Centre for Regulation of the Creative Economy (CREATe) – recorded the median income for a self-employed artist in the UK to be £12,500, about half the sum earned by a worker on minimum wage. The median was lower for artists from more challenging socio-economic backgrounds (£7,500), for women (£7,500) and for artists with disabilities (£3,750). Eighty per cent of respondents described their sources of earnings as 'unstable, or very unstable'. This was in a period when the cost of living was punishing.

---

1   A famous exception is *Beautiful Inside My Head Forever*, a two-day auction of work by Damien Hirst at Sotheby's in London which was organised by the artist himself. Taking place on 15 and 16 September 2008, the sale notoriously coincided with the collapse of the investment bank Lehmann Brothers and the start of a global economic crisis.

I have proceeded through adult life in the belief that I will, in the near future, attain another level of grown-up-ness, at which point people will behave reasonably and compensate me adequately for my work. Sometimes they do, sometimes they don't (like everyone in the art world, I am still routinely asked to work for free, despite the fact that THIS IS MY JOB, not some cute hobby). The bad news for artists is that underpayment continues into the highest levels of the public sector.

The 2023 *Structurally F—cked* report authored by the artist-run organisation Industria included data on artist fees shared anonymously.[2] One lowlight of the report was an artist paid 'a £6000 fee for 2 years working full-time on a major commission for an extra-large public institution in London', a fee that 'broke down to around £12.50 a day, or an estimated hourly rate of just £1.56'. This was not an anomaly: other artists likewise reported paltry fees for major institutional exhibitions and commissions. While the names of institutions were redacted, they were among the most important contemporary art galleries in the country – museums of global reputation – and the commissions were at a level considered career-defining.

These issues are not confined to the UK. The 2024 *Artists as Workers* report commissioned by Creative Australia found the average gross income for art workers was

---

2   This report was commissioned by a-n – The Artists Information Company – an excellent organisation serving artists in the UK. The data was collected by Industria through their Artist Leaks project, which gathered testaments on artist pay and fees through a public call-out.

A\$54,500 (£26,000). Just A\$15,300 (£7,500) of this was from arts-related activities, with the rest a combination of creative work and money from non-arts sources. In other words, living by art alone is not a reality for most artists.

In 2008, a group called W.A.G.E (Working Artists and the Greater Economy) formed in New York to agitate for artists to be paid appropriate fees (or indeed any fee) for showing in public institutions. A 2010 study by W.A.G.E revealed that 'the majority (58.4 per cent) of respondents did not receive any form of payment, compensation or reimbursement for their participation, including the coverage of any expenses' for exhibitions at venues ranging from artist-run spaces to globally recognised New York institutions. W.A.G.E has since lobbied for the payment of artist fees and offers a fee calculator for artists, among other online tools.

So, how do artists survive – what makes making art possible if they're not supporting themselves through sales? Some get by on a mixture of grants and commission fees. Some come from generational wealth or are supported by a family member (of the respondents in the DACS report, over half came from socially and economically privileged backgrounds – more than double the proportion in the general workforce in the UK). Most work part- or even full-time to support their creative work, spending just one or two days each week in the studio.

Things don't have to be like this. Ireland has trialled a Basic Income for the Arts pilot scheme, under which artists and creative practitioners were given a payment of

€325 (£285) a week. Early results for the pilot, which ran from 2022 to 2025, showed, unsurprisingly, that those on the scheme spent more time on their creative work, but also that there was a reported decrease in depression and anxiety among participants.

Mathsy interlude over. You've made it through the bad bit. Give yourself a gold star.

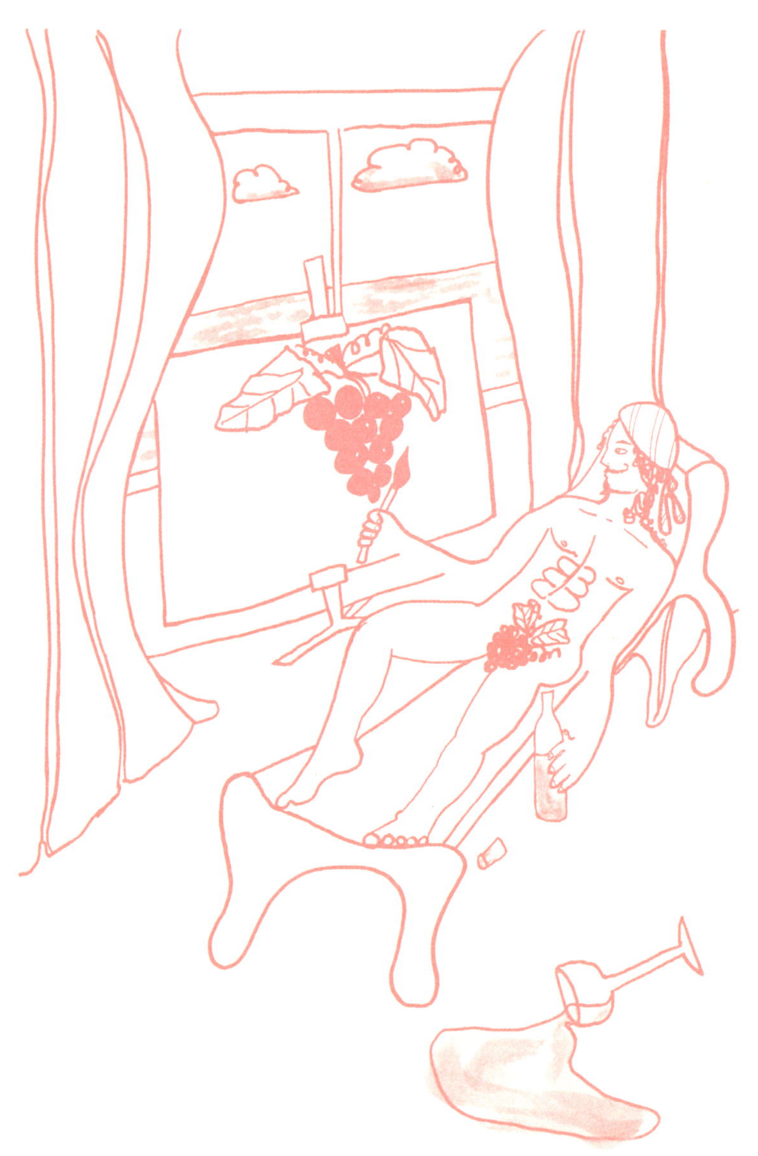

PART 1

ALTERNATE REALITIES

The conventional idea of art world success takes sales and market performance as an important metric. Only the naive and romantically deluded would deny an artist the opportunity to make money from their work. There is, however, a substantial gulf between selling work at a level that is affordable to friends and family, and the high-octane hustle required to get within paint-spitting distance of representation by an international gallery. Some artists relish the hustle (for anyone interested in that route, you'll find more in Part 7), but sales figures are not the only metric of artistic success. Not everyone can sell like Jeff Koons (not even Jeff Koons always sells like Jeff Koons), or wants to.

Part 1 invites you to take a realistic look at the art world, and the role you see for yourself in it. It also invites you to think about the kind of art world that you want to occupy, and what success might mean on your own terms.

THERE IS MORE THAN ONE ART WORLD

Storm Darragh is driving horizontal rain across the Suffolk landscape as I arrive at Asylum Studios. We're deep inside the forbidding tarmacked acreage of a decommissioned US Air Force base, 40 minutes from the nearest town. I feel like I've stepped onto the set of *Children of Men*.

This is the first Saturday in December. Seven thousand kilometres away, colleagues are enjoying an early swim ahead of Art Basel Miami Beach. On the train to Ipswich, I read their reports and social media posts, complete with celebrity sightings (Natalie Portman! Jared Leto!) and glitzy openings (Vanessa Raw at The Rubell!).

Asylum, an artist-run space and studio complex, has been running for over 25 years. My talk is in a central room that also serves as a gallery. One artist is stapling blankets over a doorway so that kids can watch a movie in an adjacent room. Another is rigging up a spotlight. There's an urn of hot water on a table beside teabags and biscuits. The audience crammed into the space includes a week-old baby and a characterful spaniel who looks like he's wearing a blonde toupee.

My invitation to Rihanna and A$AP Rocky's Art Basel Miami Beach party seems to have been dropped by the carrier pigeon, but honestly, I'd rather be in Suffolk. I no longer have the tribal tendencies that ruled my teenage years. I don't need to crave the same experiences, like the same paintings or wish to get the same things out of being in the art world as anyone else.

The cooperative, inclusive, DIY vibe of Asylum feels polar to the glitzy commercialism of Art Basel Miami Beach, yet both are broadly part of this thing we call the art world. There is common territory – perhaps some of the artists at Asylum will have work at Art Basel – but there are also conscious and important points of difference. These might include the prioritising of community over individualism, creative independence over assumed commercial appeal, slow enquiry over confected urgency.

The art world looks so different depending on your vantage point that it might be more useful to think of an art multiverse. One that can accommodate the New York gallery scene, a community printworks in Dundee, an artist squat in a Prague schoolhouse and the kitchen table at which art is made in stolen minutes around care for a family. You may feel out of sight, but you are still part of the art multiverse.

WAYS OF BEING

Let me tell you another story. This one is called *The Perfect Bohemian*. Tormented and obsessed, precociously talented, heavy-drinking, hard-partying and a fixture at sleazy clubs, the perfect bohemian has no visible source of income, yet is sharp-tongued and mocking of the wealthy who pick up his bar tab. He lives in 1890s Paris or 1950s New York or 1990s London. He is wild and undomesticated, handsome but unkept, and has a driven intensity that makes him irresistible to sexual partners. Family life, stable relationships or bourgeois comforts are not for him: nothing exists beyond days in the studio and nights on the lash. The perfect bohemian is revered by his fellow artists, bewitches critics and is fought over by collectors, who consider him a visionary genius.

The perfect bohemian is a mythic figure, but he still informs how we expect artists to live and work. When I conducted a study on artist parents, I was amazed at how many lamented the demise of bohemian status that accompanied parenthood.[3] One artist described the loss of queer capital that came with parenting. Another admitted that while she

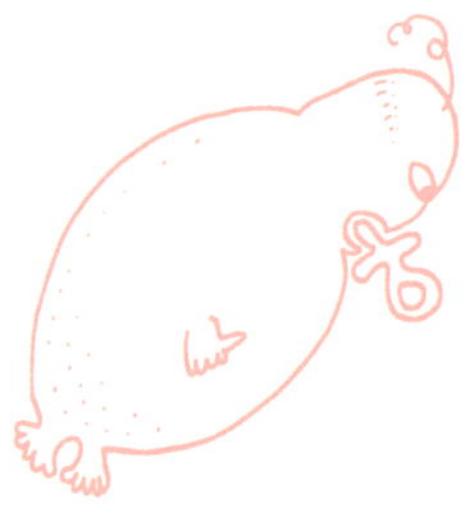

3   The study was conducted in 2019/20 and involved interviews with over 50 artist parents living in the UK. The results of the study grew into my book *How Not to Exclude Artist Mothers (and other parents)* (Lund Humphries, 2022).

had never been a party animal, the perception that as a parent she would not be available for wild nights put distance between herself and her peers.

The Perfect Bohemian has a sequel. Let's call it *The Perfect Bohemian (for the Narcissistic Era of the Camera Phone)*.

Hot and chronically online, our perfect hero is clothing averse, residing in a parallel universe in which studios come with adequate heating. No giant painting is considered complete until he has posed in front of it with a pensive gaze, the flecks on his ripped abs suggesting he painted it with his shirt off. He is having a better time than you and wants you to know it: partying with the fame adjacent, snatching selfies with celebrity friends and holidaying in exotic locales. How does he afford this lifestyle? It's unclear. Perhaps his celeb friends buy his giant paintings. Perhaps he has a property portfolio. As you drool, fume or weep over his social media feed, it can be easy to forget that your phone's screen is not a window onto real life, that this apparently perfect life is also a fiction, and one that takes tremendous energy to sustain.

Bohemian antics are catnip for biographers, tabloid reporters and social media followers, but let us be clear – the success of the Abstract Expressionists or YBAs came despite their hard drinking and heavy partying, not because of it.

Forget the myths: there is no one way to live as an artist. You can be collaborative or a loner, gregarious or introverted, quick or slow, urban or rural, commercially minded or socially focused, a marketing demon or a publicity-shy hermit. You can be a parent or a carer. You can work full-time and only enter the studio at the weekends. You can take a 15-year break during which you barely make (let alone show) any work. You are still an artist.

DEFINE SUCCESS

I was a cynic long before I entered the art world – an unimpressible, eye-rolling teen in black eyeliner. Unsurprisingly, I hold no faith in manifesting or other supernatural routes to attainment. While I may not believe in manifesting, I do know that it's impossible to attain a goal if you don't acknowledge what that goal is. So, the question I pose here is – what do you want? What would 'success' look like to you – short term, medium term or long term?

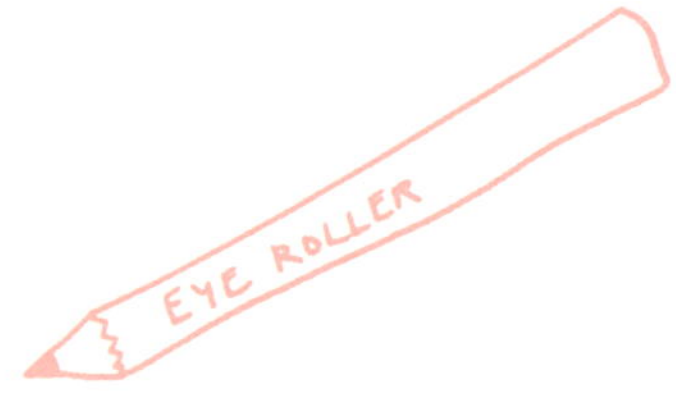

Conversations with artists suggest their notions of success change with age and experience. In early career, the idea of success can cleave most tightly to the clichés of art stardom: discovery, acclaim, gallery representation, money and celebrity. By mid-career, after witnessing or experiencing burnout, many would consider themselves successful if they could support themselves through their work or afford decent time in the studio. Later in life, thoughts turn to legacy and the possibility of having work in a public collection.

The surrealist, sex-positive multimedia artist Penny Slinger, in her late seventies at the time of writing, describes how her own understanding of success has transformed. As a young woman, she believed she was destined for fame. And she did get a taste of it, but it was fleeting. In 1971, her first solo show sold out. The art world, even then, was fickle. Her second show sold less well, and she started to look elsewhere for recognition: books, experimental theatre and film. She embarked on a spiritual path that would lead her away from the commercial art world for over 30 years. Since 1994, she has lived in California. She tells me she has a love-hate relationship with the art world, but has realised that she now needs to engage with it again.

Penny describes a spectrum of success: to express oneself freely and without limitation. To have a way for others to see and appreciate your work. To make a mark that will outlive you. To be recompensed for your work at a level that allows you to keep going. For your art to have a measurable effect on others – anything from deep liking to intense provocation. To be exhibited in a prominent institution. To be the subject of books and catalogues. To be considered a defining figure in your particular field.

Thinking of success as a series of increments is less

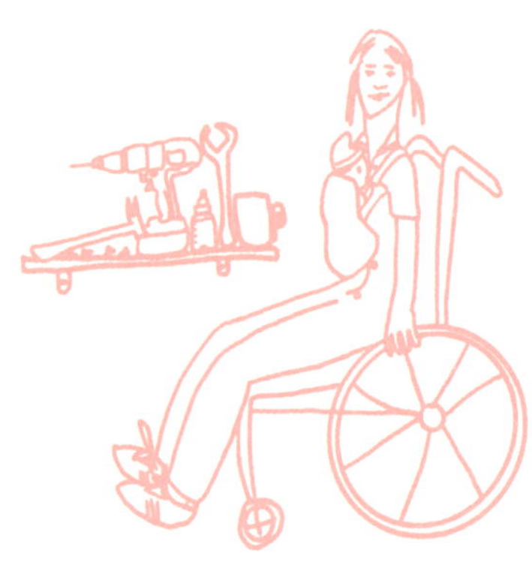

daunting. What might you achieve by next week (an organised studio?), by next month (an up-to-date website?), by next year (a group show?). I don't think anybody ever feels 'successful' – invariably, by the time a goal is achieved, another one comes into view. In setting smaller, achievable, goals, you are not only setting yourself up for incremental achievements, but you can also continue to recalibrate and shift in your ideas.

SHAPING A SUSTAINABLE CAREER

Against hyper-availability

I interviewed Ghislaine Leung in 2024 between exhibitions at the Renaissance Society of Chicago and the Kunsthalle Basel, her reputation riding high on a Turner Prize nomination. It was a good year. I'd like to say she'd taken an unconventional route to get there, but the only truly unconventional thing is that she was upfront about it.

In her poster work *Jobs* (2024), Ghislaine lists her full employment history, from 'babysitter' and 'flyer distributor' through 'art handling technician' and 'distribution manager', up to her current status as 'artist', 'lecturer' and 'mother', among other things.

The CV listed for Ghislaine on her gallery's website shows no activity as an artist prior to 2011, when she was in her thirties. Over the previous decade, her art school peers had thrown everything into showing, promoting, networking, partying and fighting to become hyper-visible and hyper-available. In other words, they did exactly what young artists are generally told to. Watching from the sidelines, Ghislaine judged that most people were only able to sustain this full-on assault for three years. As she prepared to re-engage with the art world, she pondered how an artist could achieve a 60-year career, rather than 'success' that looked perilously close to burnout.

Much of Ghislaine's work is about the labour conditions of the art world. Her approach is a performance in itself: one reflecting on how an artist might achieve an emotionally and economically sustainable career. She does not make physical objects; instead, her work exists as sets of instructions or 'scores' to be fulfilled by the gallery. 'A fountain installed in the exhibition space to cancel sound' for example, or 'child safety gates installed on all thresholds in the exhibition'. As a result, she has no studio or storage space to pay rent on. (For artists who make physical works, storage is a perpetual problem. There have been many art-works I have wanted to show after seeing old photographs of them in an artist's papers – only to discover that said artist chucked them into a skip in the 1980s.)

Ghislaine does not permit photographs or videos of herself to circulate online, removing the possibility of any kind of spectacle related to her person rather than her art. She does not do social media. Her public talks all take a Q&A format, removing the need for a prepared presenta-tion. She leaves the interpretation and preparation of her 'scores' to technical staff, so does not need to travel to install exhibitions, or even attend her own openings.

Ghislaine's work is very particular. Not all her strat-egies will be practical for other artists, but I am inspired by her focus on a sustainable career rather than flash-in-the-pan success. She is also a good reminder that artists can – and should – establish boundaries and lay down their own terms of engagement.[4]

---

4   We shall explore the question of how to establish your boundaries and terms of engagement in Part 9, p.157.

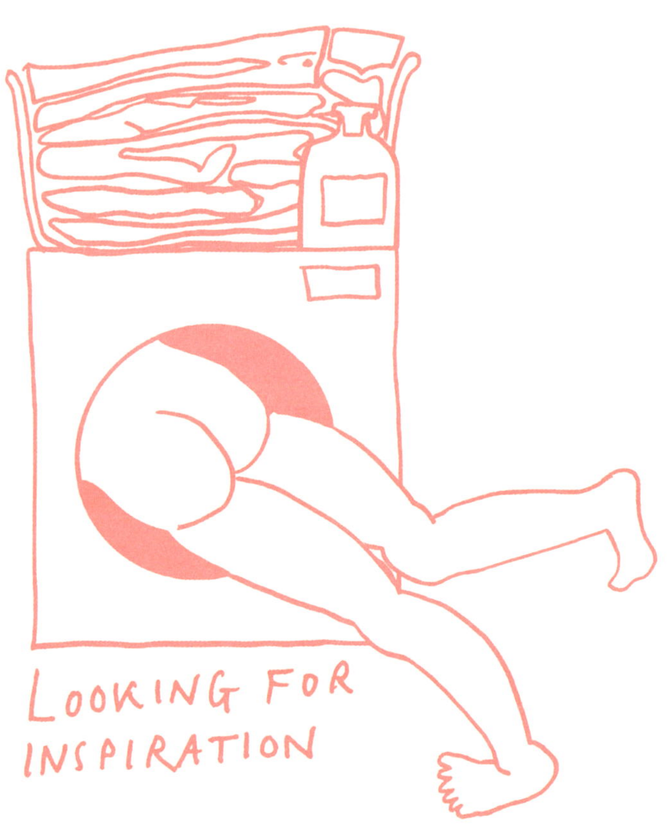

LOOKING FOR
INSPIRATION

MAKING ART

If you are reading this, odds are that you are at a transitional point as an artist. Perhaps you want to start again after a pause of many years. Perhaps you have worked steadily, slowly, privately for decades, and want to engage with the world anew. Perhaps you have been in full-time employment and finally have the time to focus on art. A great gulf may exist between all the ideas that you wish to explore, and the time and space you have available to make and experiment.

Part 2 is about your relationship to your work, the attention you afford it and the time and space you make for it. It invites you to take a critical look at your current set-up, and to work out how to make best use of what is available to you. Importantly, this is a moment for honesty, for asking whether you are making the best work you can at this moment, and what changes you can implement if not.

GETTING SERIOUS

The first and most important thing that you can do is give yourself the permission to take yourself seriously. I wince at how trite that reads, but in the years that I have been speaking on this subject, this is the key piece of advice that artists have come away with. If art has long taken second (or third) place in your life after salaried employment and caring for family, it can be quite the cognitive leap to think of yourself as an artist. This is why it is also important to acknowledge that you may need to give yourself the *permission* to do so.

Taking yourself seriously can involve small gestures, such as signing and dating your work. (This sounds trivial, but I have dealt with artists' estates where whole portfolios have been left unsigned and undated, which in turn has an impact on how the work is valued, and the likelihood that it will be acquired or accepted into a collection.) If something is worth keeping, it is worth signing and dating.

Taking yourself seriously also involves keeping proper photographic records of work, including titles, materials, dimensions and dates. If your art circulates outside a formal gallery system, you should also record who owns the work, where it is located and, if appropriate, what was paid for it. It is easy to lose track. In 2018, the Holburne Museum in Bath had to launch an appeal with Grayson Perry to track down works made between 1983 and 1994. Grayson explained that, in his early years, he relished the speed at which he could make ceramic works, which he sold 'for modest sums' and often gave away to friends. About a decade's worth of work was effectively lost to him as a result: 'I was terrible at admin and photography so kept very little record of these early pieces.'

Giving yourself the permission to take yourself seriously also involves engaging with negative feelings you may have bundled around the idea of being an artist. You may feel vulnerable, exposed, pretentious, fraudulent or in some other way ridiculous. You may feel guilty about taking time to make art, selfish for wishing to do something other than care for your family or self-indulgent for engaging in unsalaried work. Taking yourself seriously involves giving yourself permission to make time and space for art, and to draw it away from the margins and towards the centre of your life. It will also help immeasurably when it comes to talking about your work. To paraphrase that great contemporary philosopher RuPaul: if you can't take yourself seriously, how in the hell are you going to expect somebody else to?

WHAT I WEAR TO WORK

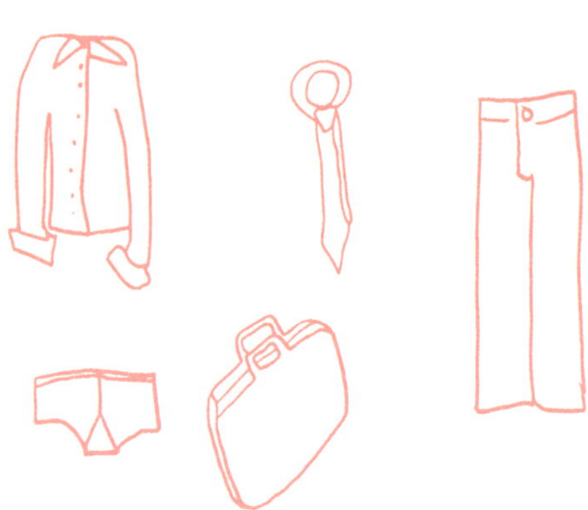

WHAT I WANT TO WEAR TO WORK

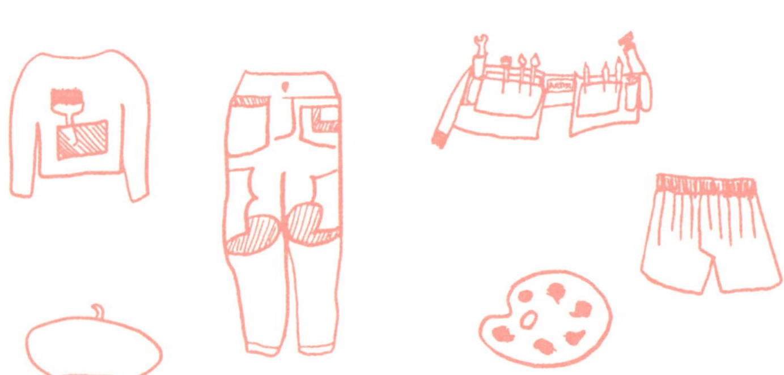

TURN UP EVERY DAY

Between 2006 and 2018, London's Serpentine Gallery hosted a series of intense 24-hour events known as 'Marathons'. Each attracted celebrated artists and thinkers who came together across their respective disciplines to explore a big idea. The theme of the 2018 edition was 'work' – a peculiarly provocative topic for artists.

One star of the Work Marathon was the painter Lynette Yiadom-Boakye – an intensely private artist who rarely gives interviews. Lynette spoke to the chef Jon Gray about what it meant to work as – and call yourself – an artist. Her parents had come to London from Ghana in the 1960s; both had trained as nurses, and for them, work meant survival. Art was, in a different way, a form of survival for Lynette. Nevertheless, she worried about the anxiety her notoriously precarious career provoked in her parents, who might have hoped their daughter had chosen a more solid and secure path.

Lynette spoke about the extraordinary discipline and work ethic of the musician Prince – an artist who treated stage and studio with the dedication a Silicon Valley entrepreneur might their start-up. He worked long hours, and the job of creativity was one he pursued every day. There was nothing apologetic about the way Prince threw himself into making art. Lynette is likewise dedicated. Both approach art as a job.

Society can struggle to consider art 'work' in the way it might tasks performed in an office environment. Art might seem a chiffon undertaking, unrelated to the weighty world of 'proper' work. Because it is pursued with passion it can be downplayed as a labour of love, undeserving of adequate remuneration (notably by wealthy collectors who invariably request discounts).

To take the work of art seriously does not mean the mood of the art itself need be serious. Prince was flamboyant, outrageous, filthy and funny. Lynette engages in wild fantasy, and indulges in quirks, habits and games in her paintings. To work like Prince is to be focused, fearless and determined, and to turn up, day after day.

PRACTICE AND PRACTICALITY

I can hear the steam whistling out of some readers' ears after that last section. Of course, it is one of the contentions of this book that the territory of art can be reclaimed – that you can step away from the art world for years and then return. Many of you reading this will be far from the point where you can imagine turning up to the studio every day. Nevertheless, it is worth having that image in mind as a vision of the dedication and commitment you should afford your work.

There is much mockery of the word 'practice' when applied to art, but I find the term useful. Perhaps you have studied yoga, tai chi, judo or karate? What all these disciplines have in common is an ethos of ongoing practice, of making certain movements or states of mind so habitual that they become ingrained. As a practitioner, you will know that restarting after a long break brings achy weeks as you reacquaint yourself with the discipline, but that your muscle memory will return. A similar phenomenon occurs with art. Any fragments of routine you can maintain in difficult years will make it easier to restart.

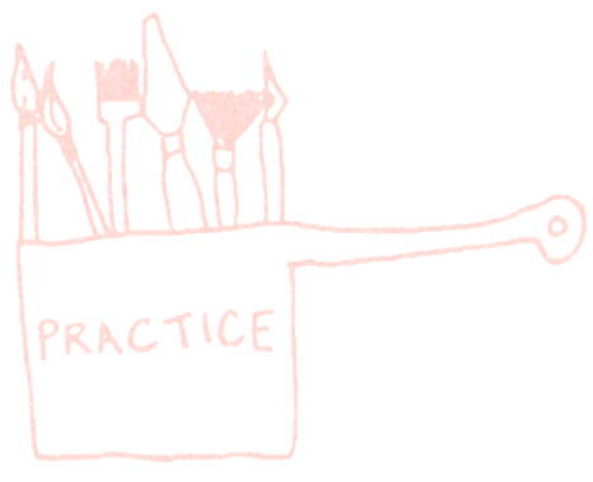

Aim to create something every day, however small. After having her first child in 1980, performance artist Bobby Baker took an unplanned eight-year hiatus from the art world. She was overstretched, caring for her children and taking on salaried work to support them. She lost confidence. Her new status as a mother undermined the sense of self that allowed her to call herself an artist. Between 1984 and 1985, Bobby undertook a project of *Timed Drawings*, one a day, each relating to the minutiae of life as a wife, mother, worker and artist. These colour drawings reflect on her mental state, domestic struggles or the small pleasures of everyday life. Some are funny, others furious. Each is made in the time available that day, which is recorded on the drawing – 30 minutes, 18 minutes, often less. Together, they fill six sketchbooks. Small gestures stack up.

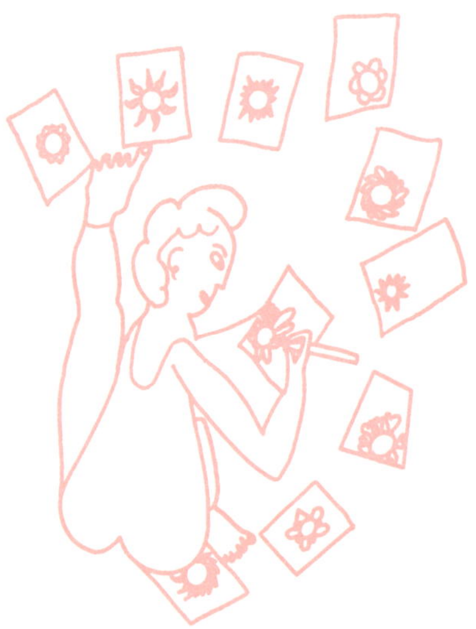

Of all the disciplines, drawing fits most easily around other elements of life – you can draw during phone calls, on public transport, sitting in a playground. A surprising number of artists draw from life every day – among them, abstract sculptor Ruth Asawa, who drew meticulous botanical studies of plants from her garden. Exhibited alongside her celebrated wire sculptures at MoMA in 2025, Asawa's plant studies show her experimenting with materials, techniques and ways of seeing across her career.

Other artists adopt the practice of 'morning pages' described by Julia Cameron in her book *The Artist's Way* (1992): three full A4 pages – no more, no less – written longhand at the start of the day. The morning pages are written as a stream of consciousness, a way to let off steam, to relieve anxiety or to explore ideas. They are, crucially, private, but might also throw out ideas worth revisiting.

If you are extremely skilled at rationalising your way out of things, being part of a group endeavour can add a helpful level of accountability. The Scandinavian Collage Museum runs an annual online 'Februllage' challenge, inviting people to make a daily collage in response to a prompt word ('vinyl', 'doubt', 'suitcase') throughout February. Similar monthly challenges – from abstract photographs to monoprints to self-portraits – are held by groups around the world. Sharing these rapidly executed exercises in a non-judgemental forum helps break down anxiety about showing your work to other people and gets you into the groove of daily practice.

Fitting drawing or writing into your everyday keeps you involved in the practice of art and can help combat lost confidence. Even if you have regular studio time, daily practice means that you've already made *something* before you've even had a chance to procrastinate.

IT'S NOT ALL ABOUT PRODUCTIVITY

It took my kids moving out of home (a.k.a. 23 years of parenthood) for me to go on a writer's residency. I was shocked and proud to have been awarded a place, and had grand ambitions for what I would achieve. On the first morning, I sat compliantly at my table ready to knock out a feverish 1,000 words, and was rendered giddy by the realisation that I didn't *have* to write anything. Indeed, it might be better if I did not. Here I was, cut off from daily life. Why plod into a routine, when I could provoke and challenge myself to think more deeply, and write more creatively? I spent days reading and arranging pictures taped to my studio walls. Bliss. Taking a break from writing changed the resulting book – it gave me the distance needed to tighten my ideas, as well as a chance to loosen up stylistically. The writing, once I did start, was more playful.[5]

If your time to make art is hard-won, the idea of doing something other than productive work can seem excruciating. You've paid rent on a studio, or arranged childcare, or endured days in a dull job to get here, and you want something to show for it. The problem with focusing on results is that we tend to attain them by accustomed

---

5   The book in question was *Acts of Creation: On Art and Motherhood* (Thames & Hudson, 2024).

routes. In other words, if we want a reliable outcome, we habitually stick to methods that we know yield results.

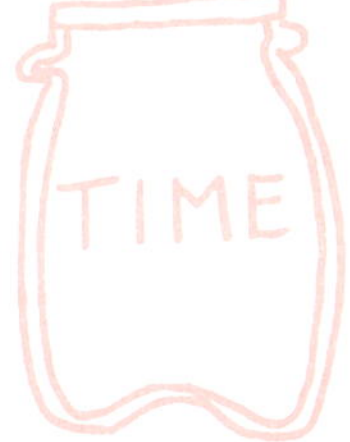

It can feel hard to justify taking time for research or speculative and high-risk work when your hours are so precious, but it is important. Without scope for experimentation – and, most importantly, failure – your work can't evolve.

SKILLING UP

An awkward conversation I try to avoid is the one where artists ask why no one will show their work. There are many dull and unpleasant reasons why this might be the case (the art world is rotten with all kinds of prejudice), but there is also a marked possibility that the work in question is not all it could be. I mean something quite specific by this. That there is a significant gulf between intention and execution. Sometimes this is the result of an idea not being thought through: the work is conceptually muddy. Quite often, though, it results from a lack of technical skill.

I often encounter artists who lean into their lack of technical skill by adopting an aesthetic that I have unimaginatively dubbed 'looks a bit shit'. There is art in the world that is wild, raw and primal because it erupted from the artist with unfiltered immediacy. This is not the same as art that 'looks a bit shit'. Art that 'looks a bit shit' has its form dictated by technical shortcomings, and not in a good way.

Let me share an open secret. Artists at the top end, the ones with technically complicated sculptures and installations in flash galleries, often work with professional fabricators. Fabricators are highly skilled and can translate a sketchy concept into a slick three-dimensional object. Maybe one day their services will be within your means. For the time being, if you fear you are an honorary member of the 'looks a bit shit' movement, it's time to skill up. Consider local adult education and evening classes (I have taken many), as well as correspondence courses and online courses.

In the business world, engaging in Continuing Professional Development is applauded. So should it be for you. Even if your work by no means 'looks a bit shit', you should still consider a refresher.

Many returning or late-starting artists go (back) to art school. You will not stick out – mature students make up a significant portion of the student body, particularly at MA level. Art school has much to offer (more on that in Part 3), but it won't be right for everyone. It's expensive.

The semesters and weekly schedules rarely correspond to children's school terms and timetables. You may not feel inclined to put yourself through the stress of application.

Fortunately, we are in a golden era of alternative art schools. These are inexpensive (in some cases free), have small class sizes and abound in mature students. Courses vary from a single term to a few years. I've taught at quite a few, and they've impressed me greatly. They may not have a flashy building (or any building at all), but students and tutors alike are diverse, engaged and motivated. As an interesting marker of the growing significance of alternative art schools in the UK's art ecosystem, many of their graduates are now eligible for New Contemporaries, the country's most significant early career award.

Alternative art schools have been around for as long as artists have fought one another, flouted convention and rebelled against institutional strictures. They are a global phenomenon – from the School of Improper Education in Yogyakarta, Indonesia, to the revered Market Photo Workshop in Johannesburg, South Africa.[6] Their flourishing is testament to the diverse routes the life of an artist might take.

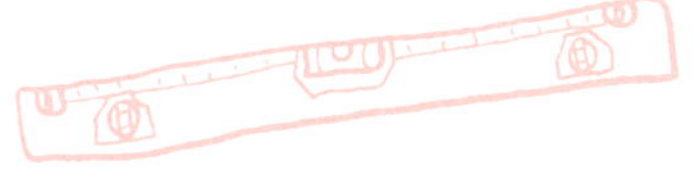

---

6   A list of alternative art schools, short courses and correspondence courses can be found on the website of artist resources that accompanies this book.

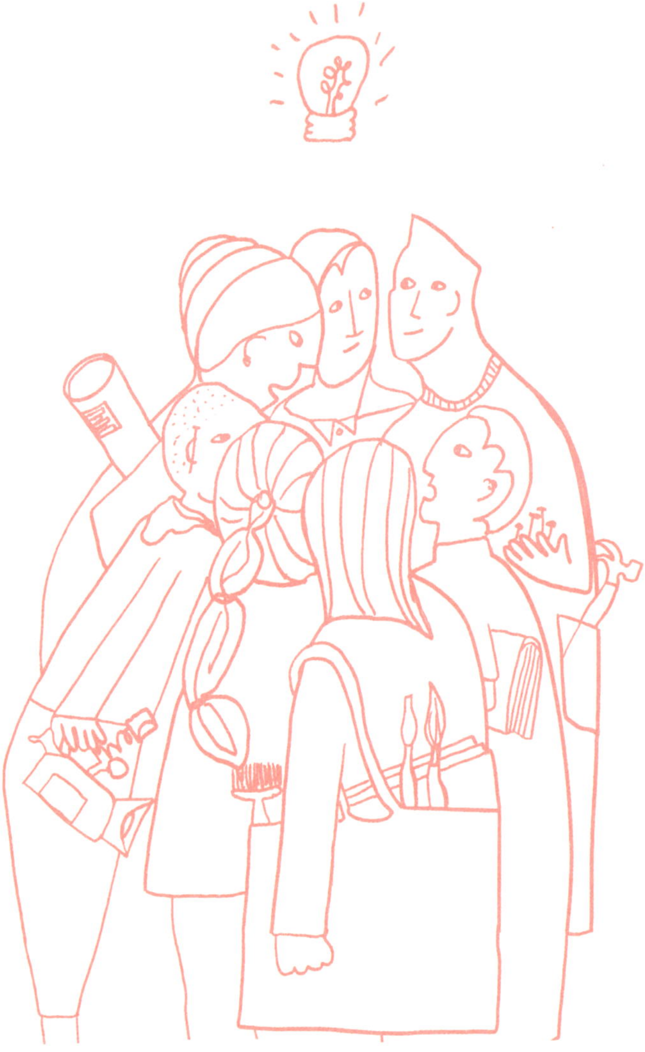

PART 3

THE EXPANDED ART SCHOOL

In the final year of the last century, I was sent by *The Times* to interview the conceptual artist, sculptor and filmmaker Cerith Wyn Evans about his solo show at Tate Britain. Not so secretly, I was more interested in asking about his social circle, which seemed to extend to every exciting person in the UK at the time. When Cerith wasn't making art or music videos, or clubbing, he played in the excellently named all-bass guitar band, Big Bottom. Two years previously, I'd watched Big Bottom play for Michael Clark in a dance work commemorating their friend, the performance artist Leigh Bowery. The whole thing was intoxicating.

Cerith told me that as a teenager growing up in Wales, he dreamed of moving to London to be an art student. I remember being struck by this specific ambition: to want to be an *art student*, rather than an artist. In the late 20th century, art schools were spaces of free experimentation, where nascent fashion designers, artists, performers and musicians reimagined the world in an edifice equipped with printmaking facilities, darkrooms and studios. Saint Martins and the Royal College of Art provided the template for Cerith's early career: collaborative, sociable and interdisciplinary.

Art schools have changed since Cerith's student years, but they still provide much more than mere education. Most importantly, they offer a peer group with a mixed skill set, strong opinions, diverse influences and a healthy degree of personal rivalry. Forget the name-check prestige and the degree show: this dynamic peer group is the prime advantage a recent graduate has over the returner or late starter. Part 3 looks at how you might create something of the art school dynamic beyond the school walls.

THE STUDIO COMPLEX

When my eldest son left home, I fumigated his bedroom for a few weeks, then moved my desk and books in. It has become my office, grudgingly ceded when he comes home for Christmas. I have space for bookish sprawl, can write at peculiar hours and face none of the distractions endured at the kitchen table. Once you have your own working space set up at home – be it office or studio – why would you want to leave?

It is rarely acknowledged how lonely making art can be. Particularly so if you work from home. If you barely step beyond the front door and seldom encounter others, you will have abundant time to work – and an ideal environment for dark and unhelpful thoughts. You might struggle to overcome problems or to find the energy to maintain good working habits. You may constantly second-guess yourself. You may feel cut off and overlooked. Most artists need a balance between time alone to work and time spent engaging with art, artists and the world.

Leaving your home set-up and moving into a studio complex isn't going to solve all your problems, but it can be transformative. Paying rent on a studio may be more than you can take on, but if you can, it is worth considering. Firstly, the financial outlay represents a commitment to take yourself seriously (remember that?). Secondly, in stepping away from the home environment, you step away from the headspace of home and towards your separate identity as an artist. Thirdly, and perhaps most importantly, in entering a studio complex, you become part of a community of artists.

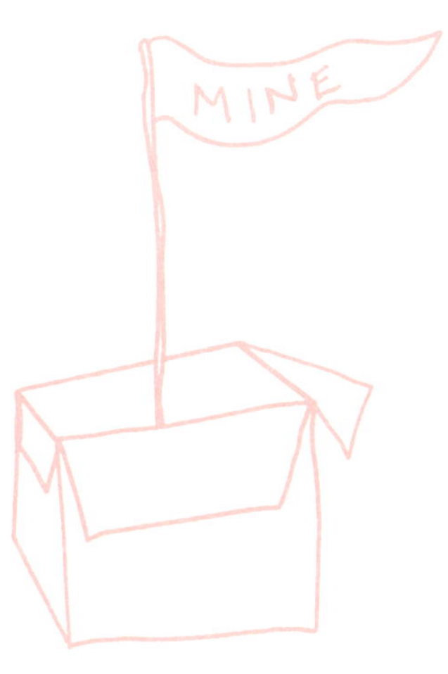

Studio complexes vary, but the best (by which I mean most dynamic, rather than most luxurious) tend to be artist-run and include a common space in which to stage small exhibitions, screenings, discussions and other events. It may be tricky to find, but this sociable and collaborative set-up is your ideal. Here you will have the chance to see what other artists are doing, to be inspired, challenged and provoked by them. Within this studio group, you may find people to discuss books and art with, to look to for feedback and perhaps even to show work alongside. It is your first step towards finding the peer group that is such an important source of support for recent graduates.

Who would leave their cosy home studio to commute to a scrappy unheated space on the outskirts of town? As it turns out, you.

THE GROUP CRIT

It is delightful to have your work praised, and praise is indeed what most people will offer, because they think it is what you want to hear. It is far more difficult to find people you respect who will give an engaged and honest response. Offering critique is exposing for both parties: the artist may feel vulnerable, and the person responding may fear causing offence, potentially damaging a friendship. Yet within the right framework, the process is invaluable, giving the artist insight into how their work is perceived by the outside world. The discussion brings aspects to light – good and bad – that the artist themself was unaware of. Writers experience this as part of the route to publication. By the time you read it, this text will have gone through multiple edits, some more brutal than others. It is never a pleasant experience, but it is necessary. And I am absolutely never a brat about it. Much.

At art school, crits are group sessions in which students present work to tutors and fellow students, who are then invited to discuss and respond in an open way. This is a process many graduates miss in the years that follow. The structure of a crit is easy to replicate in the absence of tutors. You need a willing group of artists, space to meet and an agreed code of conduct to keep things civil and constructive. (The bruising crit sessions of previous generations have become legendary. Senior staff at one art school I worked with in Belgium routinely brought students to tears. Today, callous, thoughtless and hostile behaviour is discouraged, and for good reason.)

In 2009, Kate Pickering and Charlotte Warne Thomas formed the nomadic crit group Peer Sessions after graduating from the MFA course at Goldsmiths, University of London. What started as a supportive network within London's hostile art world has evolved into a long-running public project involving hundreds of artists. Peer Sessions follows a 'silent crit' model. Two artists present their work in turn with only the barest contextual information, then listen in silence to the response of the group. Charlotte and Kate moderate the sessions, keeping the tenor constructive and respectful. The artists presenting work must be willing to perform as an engaged part of the group in other crit sessions. This is an evolving community, not a resource to be dipped into and then discarded.

There are other formats and other ways to establish groups. During the COVID-19 pandemic, ex-alumni of Central Saint Martins set up online crit sessions, with participants joining from as far afield as China, Lebanon and Pakistan. They met over a video call every couple of months to discuss work they were struggling with. Despite the distance and infrequency, the group worked well because all had emerged from the same group crit tradition.

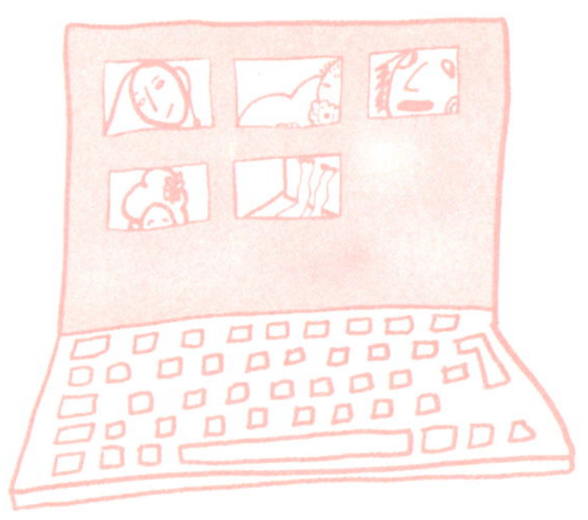

All crit groups share certain features. They are non-hierarchical: while there may be figures facilitating the session, everyone's opinion is equally valid. They are ongoing and regular – perhaps once a month – ensuring common cause, and confident discussion of one another's work. All participants should be willing to both offer and receive critique.

CURRENT IDEAS

If I need an idea to steal, I listen to artists. They are curious, well read, informed and intellectually omnivorous. The big ideas that dominate today's public conversation – from the Anthropocene to non-human intelligences to the subtleties of gender – were already being discussed by artists decades ago.

Art school curricula offer a strand drily referred to as 'theory' – a word horrifyingly suggestive of impenetrable French philosophy. The point of this theory strand is to introduce stimulating ideas. These might be about the history of art and aesthetics, but they might also connect to social and political topics such as empire, labour, feminism or AI. Beyond the lecture halls and tutorials, there is also a charged circulation of texts and references between the students, which continues after graduation. As a result, I'll often encounter waves of works inspired by a well-shared text, either new or rediscovered.[7]

It would be dreary if everyone made work engaging with the same ideas; nevertheless, it is important to be

---

7   Influential texts in recent years have included Donna Haraway's 'A Cyborg Manifesto' (1985), Frantz Fanon's *Black Skin, White Masks* (1952), and Ursula K. Le Guin's *The Carrier Bag Theory of Fiction* (1986).

47

aware of the current discourse. It will introduce new ways of seeing the world, help you better engage with the art of your peers and perhaps lead you in unexpected directions. One of the best ways of doing this is to join – or start – a reading group. (A reading group is not the same as a book group. In a book group you are expected to read a book in advance of the session; in a reading group a short text is read aloud during the session and then discussed. Typically, participants sit in a circle, reading paragraphs in turn.)[8]

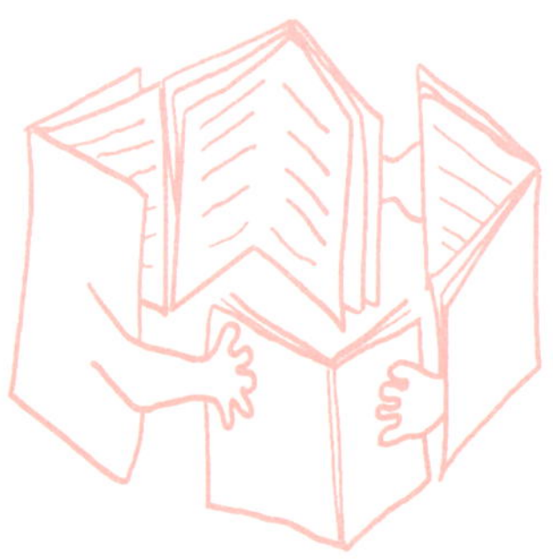

Reading groups can be formed around a tight theme, led by experts who select the texts: the Feminist Duration Reading Group was started by Helena Reckitt in 2015 to explore Italian feminist texts of the 1970s and '80s, for example. They can also be collaborative and general, with members taking it in turns to select readings. Be gentle and keep an open mind – this format crumbles if participants are

---

8   If English is not your first language, or you are dyslexic, or find reading off the page a challenge, don't panic – this is not a public performance, it's a way to engage as a group. Everyone will have their own print-out of the text so they can follow along.

unceremoniously dismissive of one another's selections. The texts don't need to be theoretical – you might choose a short story by Franz Kafka, an extract from a novel by Samuel Beckett or a poem by Audre Lorde. It is up to you how often to meet. A tightly themed season might favour weekly sessions. An ongoing collaborative group might instead meet monthly.

GUIDANCE

In Homer's *Odyssey*, the goddess Athena assumes the form of King Mentes (or Mentor) to guide Telemachus, son of Odysseus, in his father's absence. As the art world has increasingly professionalised, mentors have become an established part of the landscape. Alas, few offer the wisdom of Athena, but it's easy to see the appeal. Most artists work alone, with little to steer them save crummy 'how to' guides. A mentor is a senior figure who will engage with your work, offering advice, guidance and perhaps professional connections, not unlike a good tutor.

Mentoring is similar to coaching. Both are resources for when you are feeling stuck or struggling to manage change. As a broad distinction, a coach encourages you to search for solutions within yourself, while a mentor provides guidance derived from their own experience. Professional mentors may also offer coaching, workshops, lectures and other developmental resources.

A befuddling range of people and organisations now offer more or less specialised mentoring to artists. There are professional mentors who provide career guidance to those exploring commercial representation or wanting a boost within the industry. There are working artists, writers and curators who offer mentoring alongside their own creative practice. Some mentors take a spiritual or holistic approach, offering something closer to therapy. Others are academic and businesslike. Some approaches will sound ickier to you than others. Ask around and search for a good match, then request an initial chat before committing to a months-long mentoring programme.

If you are looking for help with something special-ised – collaborating with scientific institutions, developing a socially engaged practice, publishing a photo book – you can also contact someone in the field and ask whether they would mentor you.

Professional mentors and other self-employed arts professionals will generally expect a fee for mentorship. It is now standard for mentoring sessions to occur online. If you need a mentor to be available for a studio visit to look at your work, you should discuss this upfront and check it is something they can offer.

Finding a good mentor/mentee fit is important for both parties – even when they are paid, most mentors do it because the process is rewarding, so it will also be frustrating for them if they are unable to provide you with the feedback or information you need. It is important for the mentee to enter the process with good intentions. My worst experiences as a mentor have come when the mentee has signed up as a box-ticking exercise to boost their CV and has no interest in engaging properly.[9]

In 2022, Jo Harrison and I cofounded the Art Working Parents Alliance (AWP), a supportive network for parents working in the visual arts in the UK. Among other things, we match members in mentorship pairings. Parents returning to work often lack confidence and need support. The hierarchical mentor/mentee dynamic within these pairings often relaxes into a peer-to-peer relationship – something closer to a work friendship. If you are after a sounding board and some support, rather than specific career advice, peer-to-peer mentoring can work well and has the bonus of being free.

THE IMPORTANCE OF PLAY

When I speak with artists about their time at art school in the late 1960s and '70s, I am struck by how open everything was. They might have enrolled because they enjoyed painting, but within weeks they found themselves involved in

---

9   I should not need to tell you that mentoring sessions with a curator or critic are not an open licence to pitch them. Just. Don't.

experimental cinema or performance. Perhaps they returned to painting at the end of the course, but those years of free experimentation contributed to who they were and what they ended up doing. I am not suggesting you plunge into three years of casual sex and recreational drugs, but there is a lot to learn from the freewheeling vibe of art school at its most radical. At the Bauhaus of the 1920s, and Black Mountain College – an experimental North Carolina liberal arts school – in the 1940s, there was no clear border between art and life. Everything was available to be reimagined, whether that involved breaking down the supposed distinction between the fine and applied arts, collaborating on entertainments or trying out skills from origami to mime.

It is freeing to push yourself into uncomfortable territory, to take risks that might open you to ridicule, and not to care what anyone thinks. I know one artist in her fifties who undertook a punishing six-month exercise regime so that she could dance in one of her video works, and another who formed an art punk band. You don't need to do anything so terrifying, but you might experiment with a new medium (Printmaking? Photography?) or collaborate with someone in a different discipline (Sound? Dance?). The point is not to create the greatest work of living genius, but to stretch yourself, and be stimulated by the process.

Playing with a medium in which you lack mastery reminds you that if things don't go to plan, it's not a catastrophe – you can move on. Play is a way of learning. At Black

Mountain College, Ruth Asawa created abstract compositions using the school's laundry stamp. I have a print made by another sculptor while she was experimenting with the nursery school technique of potato printing. I also know a celebrated artist who acquired a passion for pottery painting workshops, of the type popular for children's parties. What is interesting, looking at the mugs and plates she paints, is that she's thought carefully about how to introduce an image to a three-dimensional object. It's a bit of fun, but it's also a problem-solving exercise.

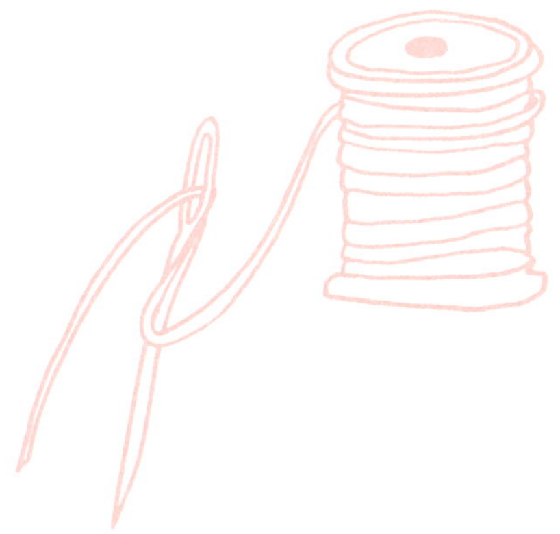

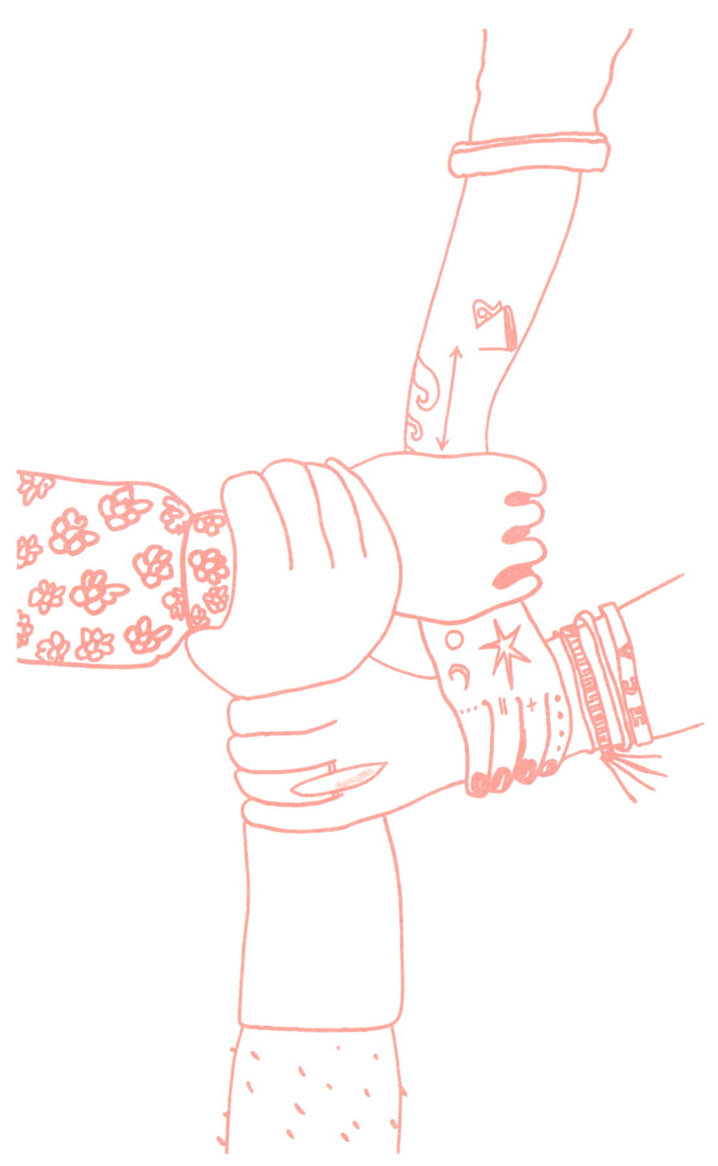

PART 4

PLUGGING IN

Art history, as written in the 20th century, celebrated the artist as lone genius. We have an image of the great artist labouring in isolation and miraculously being discovered by a dealer who champions his work and sets him on a path to global stardom. This is yet another of the art world's tall tales. There were whole communities of friends, lovers and fellow artists surrounding each of these supposed lone geniuses, and many of their most important ideas emerged from conversations, arguments and encounters. Hilma af Klint's pioneering abstract series *Paintings for the Temple* (1906–15) has its roots in regular seances during which she engaged in automatic drawing with a group of women known as The Five. Wassily Kandinsky's radical experiments were inspired by intense conversations about art, colour and spirituality conducted with a group that included his partner, Gabriele Münter, a fellow painter and avant-garde pioneer.

Artists who found recognition in their own time will have been part of a loose network that included dealers, patrons, collectors, curators and critics. There is understandable appetite for stories of rivalry and low behaviour between artists, but you can search for that in the library. Part 4 is instead about supportive friendships. Flourishing in the art world will require connections, and the key to making good ones is to remember that the benefits don't only flow in one direction: it is about offering as well as receiving.

WORKING TOGETHER

If you live in a large, expensive city and view the art world through the prism of the market, it can be easy to slip into a mindset that places you in competition with your peers. I would suggest that is a lonely place to be. I would also suggest it is not the best route to a flourishing career. You may, in addition, struggle to find people who want to go to the pub with you.

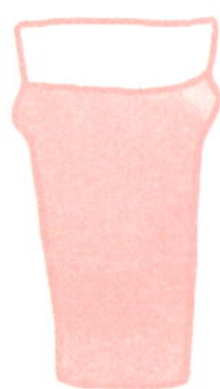

Of all the (many) artists whose careers are a testament to generosity of spirit, I am particularly moved by Lubaina Himid. From her earliest career, she supported and promoted the work of Black and Asian women, curating exhibitions including *The Thin Black Line* at London's Institute of Contemporary Arts in 1985. For over two decades, her painting career took a back seat to her work in academia. Lubaina returned her focus to public exhibitions in the 2010s, won the Turner Prize in 2017, and has since used her platform and influence to bring attention to other artists, among them Ingrid Pollard and Claudette Johnson. Honoured with a solo show at Tate Modern, she chose to share the billing with her partner and collaborator, Magda Stawarska.

Far from damaging her career, Lubaina has placed herself at the heart of a dynamic milieu. She has had a transformative impact on other artists and changed British art history. I imagine she does not lack people who want to go to the pub with her.

Much is made of that fabled phenomenon, networking. Most artists will say they are rubbish at it, but what do we actually mean when we talk about networking for artists? Artists are not tech entrepreneurs hustling for start-up funding. They're not going to be placed in a room full of suits and lanyards and expected to deliver an elevator pitch. Networking for artists is really just about being connected to other people – by which I mean the people around you, artists in your area, at your studio, visiting the same exhibitions, taking the same courses, attending the same talks.

Connections work best if the energy flows both ways. Creating meaningful, mutually supportive connections can include small gestures: sharing information about opportunities, helping others install their work, turning up for events, working collaboratively. Artists who recognise the importance of supportive connections share what they can, whether that involves writing reference letters for other artists' grant applications or running not-for-profit exhibition spaces.

OTHER KINDS OF NETWORKING

Supportive Connections

There is a global ecosystem of artist associations. Among them are local groups and national groups.[10] Some can be grand; others are punky upstarts. There are associations founded around a discipline or medium, such as the National Society of Painters in Casein and Acrylic in the United States. There are also organisations supporting specific groups, such as the Institute of International Visual Arts (Iniva), founded by cultural theorist Stuart Hall, which works largely with British-based visual artists of Asian and African descent. Some art schools have alumni associations – University of the Arts London has dozens, including four in mainland China.

Each performs in its own way and has its particular mission, but at base, these organisations are designed to support artists – to connect you to your fellows, to form a network within which to exchange information and to create opportunities for exhibition.

---

10 The former include groups local to a city, such as the Bath Society of Artists, or to a region, such as Arts Alliance Illinois; the latter include the Artists' Association of Finland and Federation of Canadian Artists. A working list of both local and national associations can be found on the resources website.

Most associations were founded by artists. In 2013, Simon Carter and Robert Priseman founded Contemporary British Painting (CBP) to address a lack of serious engagement with the medium. Membership is by invitation only, but any painter can sign up to CBP's newsletter, enter their annual prize or submit a work to be the Painting of the Day shared on Instagram. Nomination to CBP is based on a combination of merit and engagement. They want members to be involved with what they are doing as a group – submitting work, visiting exhibitions, participating in the wider conversation. I was one of the judges of the CBP Prize in 2022, and it was notable how familiar members were with one another's work, and that of the artists nominated for the prize. As a volunteer-led group interested in generating opportunities for fellow members, CBP offers a model for a good artist network.

We all carry discreet snobberies. It's easy to look at an artist association and feel it is not for us. That the members are too old or too young, too conservative or too radical, too numerous or too few, too chaotic or too rule-bound, that they are not like me and will not like me. Get over yourself and give it a try. The worst thing that can happen is that you waste a membership fee and a few boring evenings. You may find yourself surprised. Most associations will recognise that their ongoing existence depends on evolving to meet the needs of new members. Change may be necessary, but the catalyst for that change can be you.

In Part 4 I want to keep moving away from the idea

that networking is all about promoting your own work and self-interest. A good network is founded on bonds of mutual support and respect, on interest in other artists' work and the investment of time and effort. That is the kind of networking offered by artist associations.

YOUR FIRST INSTITUTIONAL RELATIONSHIP

Most districts will have a local arts venue. It might be as humble as a community centre or a room in the local library. It could be a Victorian art gallery or a modern edifice founded by a local benefactor. There are the most surprising institutions out there if you have the curiosity to seek them out. They offer interesting opportunities to a dynamic creative spirit with an open mind. Almost all of them will have a remit to support or connect with local artists, which means that you will be of interest to them, if they are of interest to you.

Local engagement can take you to surprising places. Elsa James was born in London but moved to Essex when she started a family. She started art studies in her thirties as a mother of two, commuting to the Chelsea College of Arts in the evenings. At a certain point, she realised that she was taking all her cultural cues from London and started to engage with her identity as a Black woman living in Essex.

She became part of the Essex Girls Liberation Front, and turned up to art events wearing a T-shirt reading 'This Is What an Essex Girl Looks Like'.[11]

In her art, Elsa researches the histories of Black women who made a mark on Essex. She has also become involved with local institutions. Metal is an arts organisation she passed many times in a local park in Southend before knocking on the door and introducing herself. That first conversation led to a five-month residency organised by Metal in 2017, and Elsa's first solo show *Forgotten Black Essex* in 2018. Her second solo exhibition was also in Southend, at the Focal Point Gallery. It attracted press attention, and her work went on to be included in a group show at Gagosian Gallery.

If you work for an arts organisation, the people who are interested in what you are doing and who want to get involved can be the best part of your job. Some amazing initiatives have emerged from informal approaches. Some years ago, the Barber Institute in Birmingham started collaborating with a local medical college, using paintings in their collection to assist with the discussion of death as part of end-of-life care. This extraordinary enterprise all started when a professor of nursing from the medical college struck up a conversation about death in art during a public event at the gallery.

As with all the relationships and networks discussed in Part 4, these are connections that work best when reciprocal.

---

11   In the UK, 'Essex Girl' is an outdated pejorative, denoting a woman characterised as unintelligent, promiscuous and materialistic. According to the old stereotype, an Essex Girl would be a white woman with blonde hair.

Marching into a local arts organisation, pronouncing yourself an undiscovered local genius and demanding a solo show is not the way to go. Attend exhibitions and events, get a sense of the mood of the place and become part of its local community. While she now shows internationally, Elsa James is still involved with Metal, working as an artist advisor to global majority artists.

RE/CONNECT

Dust off your old address book

Watching contemporaries progress to magnificence does not always bring out our most attractive qualities. It is possible to be proud of old friends while simultaneously struggling to keep feelings of jealousy, anger, resentment and bitterness in check. It is easy to feel forgotten and left behind, and to sink into a cycle of self-loathing. The path of your life may have diverged from your more illustrious contemporaries, but this is a good moment to think about reconnecting with people. You have nothing to lose but your pride.

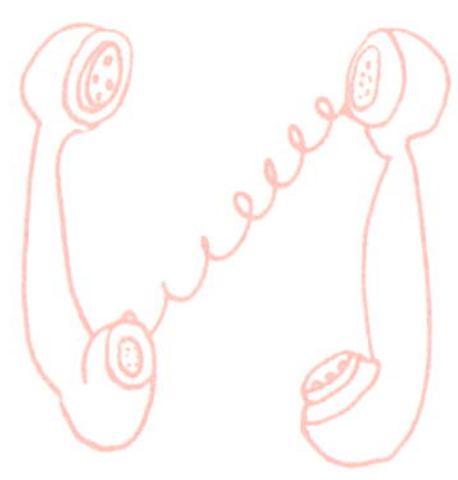

In the autumn of 2022, I held a public conversation on re-entering the art world and invited various artists to share their experiences.[12] I particularly wanted to hear from the sculptor Permindar Kaur, who seemed a perfect example of an artist who had reconnected with people after taking a break. Permindar had a flourishing career in the 1990s, with solo shows in Sweden, Spain, Canada and the UK. After becoming a mother early the following decade, she stopped making art for ten years. When she returned to the studio, she started slowly, revisiting her notebooks and exploring old ideas. She also started to sound out old contacts. One was a curator at a regional museum who had been interested in a solo show of her work before her career break. She contacted him to see if he was still there: he was, and it turned out that he was still interested.

For a later solo show in London, she approached curator and cultural theorist Eddie Chambers to write a catalogue essay. They had crossed paths in the UK in the 1990s. He was now Professor of Art and Art History at the University of Texas with dozens of publications to his name. The art world is fast-moving, so a link to a respected figure like Eddie Chambers is an effective way to catch people's attention. Permindar told me that she contacted many people she knew from her earlier career. Some did not reply, but a few did. That was enough to make a difference.

---

12   The discussion on re-entering the art world was part of a weekend festival at TJ Boulting gallery that coincided with the launch of *How Not to Exclude Artist Mothers (and other parents)*. That discussion in turn laid the foundation for this book.

I have been on the receiving end of emails from Permindar and think the tenor of her approach well judged. It works for both people she knows and people she does not. She is unselfconsciously bold in the people she contacts, but does so in a straightforward way, with neither flattery nor apology. If she wants something she will ask for it, but there is no expectation, no sense of entitlement, no endless follow-ups, no harassment. Two or three times a year she sends an update on her work to people she thinks might be interested.

CONNECTING THROUGH SOCIAL MEDIA

Instagram has changed the art world. Twenty years ago, to find new work and interesting shows, you had to read a magazine. Today, collectors and curators are more likely to discover artists and their work over social media. This has been catastrophic for the publishing industry, for writers and the health of art criticism, but in many ways has been liberating for artists. Every artist can now offer a window onto their practice, observe what their peers are up to and connect with them. They can follow the activities of curators, critics, writers and collectors, and engage in a broader online conversation. Artists living beyond the global art capitals, and those who cannot be physically present at gallery events, have a virtual view into current exhibitions, a platform on which to show their work and a way to get or stay connected.

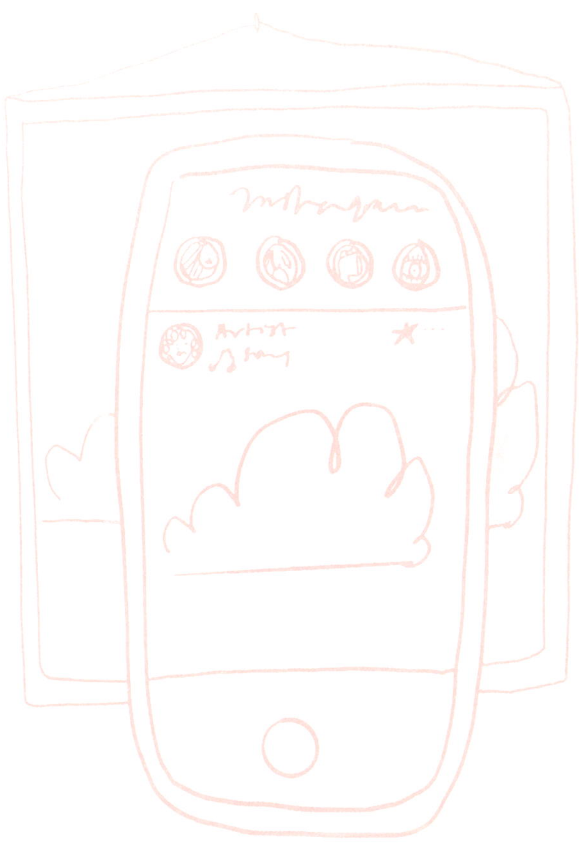

A further transformation came in 2020, when Matthew Burrows set up the Artist Support Pledge during the COVID-19 pandemic. Participating artists posted images of work priced no higher than £220 or equivalent. For every £1,100 of work they sold, they pledged to buy a work by another artist participating in the scheme. The Support Pledge was created as a sustainable economic model for artists at a time when physical exhibitions were not possible. It has had unforeseen impact, opening Instagram up as a respectable art marketplace. The imposed transparency removed pervasive squeamishness around sales – there is now less taboo around open pricing. A knock-on effect was that a whole tranche of the population realised they could afford art. It also became clear that even artists who seemed to be doing well were very short of money and used the scheme as an important source of income. As far as I can tell, there have been no ill effects for the artists – at least two that I bought work from in this period have since picked up swanky gallery representation. Many artists have subsequently made a habit of offering affordable editions or works on paper for sale over Instagram.

There is plenty of advice out there on how to manage your presence on Instagram. The hustle culture art-business bros argue that your page should be all about promoting *your* brand, and that you should only post *your* work, *your* process, *your* exhibitions and *yourself*. Personally, I appreciate artists sharing one another's work – it's often how I find interesting new people. I also enjoy reference images that give insight into the way an artist sees the world. And dogs in studios.

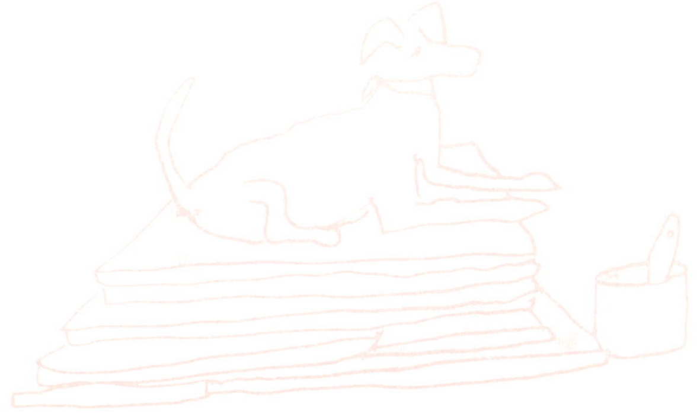

You might drive yourself mad trying to second-guess what the algorithm will promote. Prior to 2015, when Instagram only carried square images, dealers were rumoured to be sending painters on their roster square canvases to optimise their screen appeal. At the time of writing, the algorithm favours moving images over stills. By the time this book is in your hands, who knows where we'll be. Photograph your work as well as you can, post as regularly as you can bear to and interact with other people as you would hope to be interacted with yourself. For sanity's sake, take time off, and remind yourself that what you see of others' lives is as tightly edited as what you offer of your own. I assume I am not the only one who shares my successes but rarely advertises my rejections.

NEWSLETTERS AND WEBSITES

I am frequently asked whether I have an email newsletter. I do not, in part because it involves unpaid work, and in part because I find it enough to publicise engagements on social media (which also involves unpaid work yet feels less of a faff). However, I receive several artist newsletters and think they're a good tool if pitched right. They should be short, conversational, well designed and not too frequent. Quarterly is enough, though many send them monthly. Newsletters are a way to share details of upcoming exhibitions, recent excitements and developments in your work. You can also offer editions for sale.

Some artists distribute a newsletter through Patreon or other subscription platforms. This allows people to support your practice through a small monthly payment. In addition to the newsletter, you can offer higher subscription tiers through which supporters receive editions or exclusive content. Subscriptions take work – you must commit to getting a regular newsletter out, among other things – but can be particularly important for artists regularly censored on social media.

At the time of writing, the social media landscape is in turmoil. Up until very recently, I would have said that if you had a lively, regularly updated Instagram page and a quarterly newsletter, you didn't need much by way of a website. Today, I would suggest that over-reliance on any one social media platform is a risk. I have seen artists' accounts taken down because their work featured nudity. I have seen others lose a decade of posts because they were hacked. Fake lookalike accounts are popping up with ever-greater frequency. Many people have stepped away from social media platforms for political reasons.

A website can be simple, made using a generic template: a homepage with basic information, photographs of your work with dates and titles, links to any shows you've been in, and a contact form.

If you wish to draw attention to a career of long duration, particularly one in danger of being overlooked, you should put time into creating a more comprehensive record of your work online. In this case it is important to offer an archival overview, organised decade by decade, with as many links and as much bibliographical information as you can provide. It will be important for anyone coming across your work for the first time online to understand it in context and be appropriately humbled.

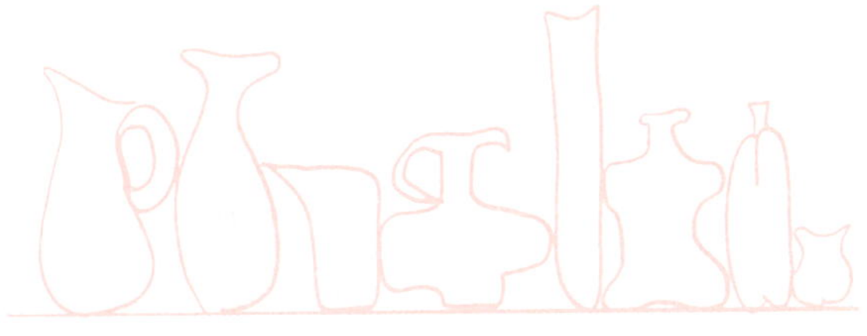

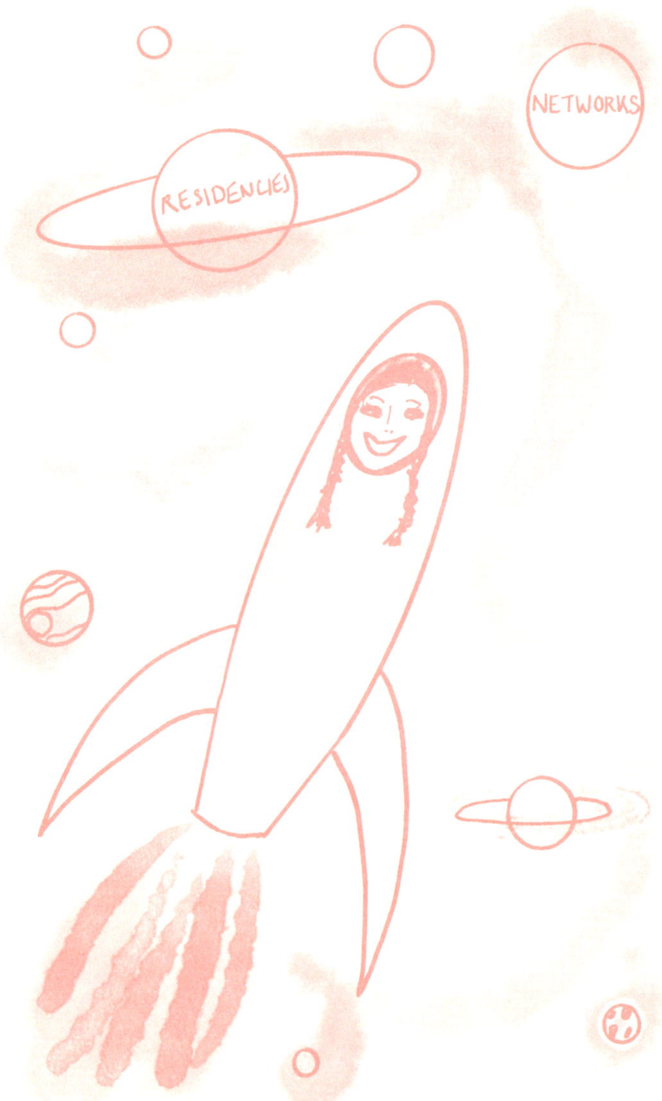

RESIDENCIES
NETWORKS

PUTTING YOURSELF OUT THERE

Decades ago, when I was the editor of a Belgian magazine, we ran an edition called 'Faking It'. There was a photoshoot on a convincing fake band, fake politician, fake socialite and fake artist, and we commissioned insiders to give anonymous intel on blagging your way through each field. Personal connections, physical attractiveness and a memorable name all helped, but the depressing revelation was that almost no-one has confidence in their own judgement. Each industry depended on a combination of hype, gossip and herd instinct to work out who was going to be the next big thing.

You could look at this from another perspective. Once you receive an endorsement from one respected source, others will likely follow.

Putting yourself out there can be alarming. Be inspired by Newcastle sculptor and drag king Lady Kitt. Kitt has a drag character called Hot Art Dad. As a disabled artist and parent, Hot Art Dad has much in common with Kitt, but rather than worrying that he might be considered difficult to work with, he sees himself as an attractive proposition both personally and professionally. As Kitt says, 'He's an egotistical wanker for sure, but it works for him –

he says what he wants and, generally, gets it.' Hot Art Dad has inspired Kitt to explore what they dub the 'wanker tipping point', to push themself to be more upfront and self-assured. You can likely be a great deal bolder in putting yourself out there than you think you can before crossing the wanker tipping point.

Part 5 is about emerging beyond your mutually supportive network into a comparatively competitive world. Younger artists have an advantage here, since there is a whole network of grants, residencies and competitions specifically aimed at those under 40. Shocking. Almost as though these organisations don't care that artists of all ages need a few shiny things on their resumé.

STUDIO VISITS

You're making work that you are proud of. Now you need to get it in front of the right people. The best way for your work to be seen is on exhibition (we'll dive into that in Part 6, p.85), but timing and geography do not always make this possible. In which case you can propose a studio visit.[13]

---

13   It is not an issue if you work from home rather than a formal studio. Anyone who regularly makes studio visits will be well used to being with artists in their homes, with their pets and family members knocking around. The only exception could be hosting visits for groups, which may be impractical if you are, for example, working at a small table in your kitchen.

Studio visits happen throughout your career. It can feel odd to have your private workspace invaded. Arrange as many visits as you can with people you know early on to get used to them. If you are very nervous, do trial visits with family and close friends. You are inviting people into your space, so the onus is on you to make them feel welcome and relaxed.

Start off by hosting an artist you'd be excited to share your new work with (they may wish to reciprocate). If you have a mentor, invite them to view your work and offer feedback. In Part 4, I suggested becoming involved with your local art centre (p.60) – once you have met them a few times, invite the programmer, director or curator. If someone you admire professionally has engaged with your work in a meaningful way on social media, an invitation to visit your studio is a good next step.

Further on in your career, visitors can include anyone who has bought your work, friendly curators, interested journalists and gallerists. Most reasonably senior people in the art world will only make a studio visit if they are interested in your work, but don't assume a visit represents a commitment to anything more. You may also be approached to host groups of collectors led by an art advisor or curator. In this instance, your studio is performing somewhat as a tourist destination: negotiate a fee with the person organising the visit and discuss with them how to structure the event.

A visit usually lasts around an hour. You will need a

clean chair for your guest (they should leave your studio with inspiration, not indelible art goo on their coat), and the wherewithal to make them a cup of tea. (If you are visited by a group, forget the tea, but make sure there's a chair or two for the less mobile.) Most importantly, you should plan what you want to show, arrange your studio so that you can access the works in order, and have things to say about each one.

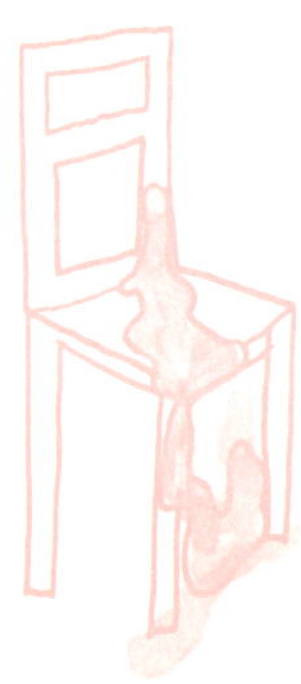

I hereby issue an apology on behalf of the art multiverse for any visitors who make this a weird experience. Collectors in particular may be on unfamiliar territory and ask invasive questions or offer unsolicited advice. I've encountered people on group studio visits who look bored to be there, talk among themselves, remain stuck to their phone screens and only engage with the artists to demand a selfie at the end. They will be a tiny minority. Most people will be excited to visit your studio, recognising it as a privileged opportunity to engage with you and your work.

GRANTS

Grants are financial allocations awarded to artists or arts organisations. They can be awarded by public bodies, such as the regional UK arts councils or the National Endowment for the Arts, or by private trusts and foundations. You need to apply for them, and the selection process is competitive. Arts Council England's popular Developing Your Creative Practice (DYCP) grant has application rounds three or four times a year and receives around 2,000 submissions to each – only 20 per cent of which are successful.

Every grant-giving body has its own priorities, and each grant carries specific criteria.[14] Many funding bodies have a bespoke application form, but even if they do not, you should not assume that you can send the same generic letter with each grant application.

Have a specific objective or project in mind and then identify potential funding sources that match it, rather than vice versa. Your objective need not be grand or complicated: far better if its easily explained with a clear outcome. Many

---

14 The Pollock-Krasner Foundation grant, for example, 'provides financial resources for visual artists to create new work, acquire supplies, rent studio space, prepare for exhibitions, attend a residency and offset living expenses', but cannot be used to fund academic study or personal travel. Its definition of 'visual artists' is specific – filmmakers and performance artists need not apply.

of the strategies mentioned earlier in this book are eligible for grant funding, including short technical courses, mentoring and digitising archival material. Apply well in advance of the project date, anticipating that your application may be refused – at which point you can ask for feedback, make appropriate changes and resubmit it on the next deadline. It may take a few rounds of rejections, feedback and resubmissions for an application to be successful.

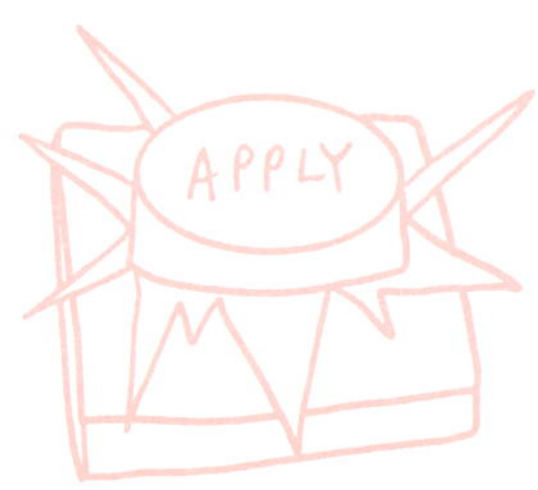

Grants are crucial to artists with a less commercial practice – those who work in the public sphere, whose projects are rooted in the community or who are otherwise socially engaged. This is reflected in the distribution of grants, a large proportion of which are directed towards the support of identified social groups.

Many application forms use obscure bureaucratic language and are poorly written. If you really struggle to complete these forms, some funding bodies, including Arts Council England, now offer access support for applicants who are deaf, disabled or neurodivergent.

You may be asked to list a referee or provide a letter

of endorsement from an arts professional. This needs to be someone who knows you – perhaps a recent visitor to your studio. Give anyone you approach for a letter of recommendation a couple of weeks' notice and have a back-up plan.

All of this takes time. It can be frustrating, a great deal of fuss for modest financial results. No one enjoys rejection, but anyone who applies for grants will have experienced it. I have my own star-studded list of knock-backs, but those grants that I have been awarded were a huge boost. Over and above the financial support, they showed that someone believed in me. To be awarded a grant is an important marker.

OPEN CALLS AND JURIED SHOWS

The oldest open submission show in the world is the Royal Academy Summer Exhibition in London, held annually since 1769. Anyone who registers in time and pays the entry fee (£40 per work, at the time of writing) can submit for consideration. The total number of submissions is capped at 18,000. Applicants first send digital images, from which a maximum of 4,000 works are selected for the next round. These must be physically delivered to the Royal Academy for presentation to the selection committee hanging that year's show. Their choices are idiosyncratic, led by the

Academicians' interests or their plan for the galleries (in 2022, one Academician selected all the pictures of clouds, which he hung on a single wall). The show itself is vast – over 1,700 works in 2025 – and receives hundreds of thousands of visitors.[15]

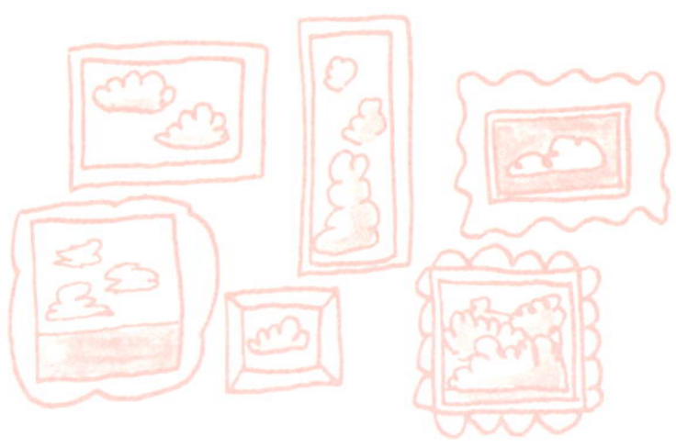

The costs and odds of inclusion in the RA Summer Exhibition offer a useful benchmark when judging the criteria of open call or open submission shows (also known as juried exhibitions in the United States). Many are respected, but some are distinctly iffy. We will delve into exploitative practice further in Part 10 (p.172), but in considering open calls I would exercise caution and judgement.

Artists dislike paying entry fees, but they have a purpose. Selecting works for a show is arduous and even a low fee deters time-wasters. The fee helps cover the costs, which include months of truly dull admin work, hanging and lighting an exhibition, staffing the venue and printing materials. Good open calls are held by arts societies and regional

---

15 The RA Summer Exhibition includes works by Academicians and invited artists as well as open submissions, so the likelihood of your work being selected is much lower than might appear from these figures.

organisations wanting to support artists. There should be a reasonable payoff between the entry fee, the prestige of the exhibition itself and the chance of your work being selected.

Smell a rat if you encounter high entry fees, an open call without a clear selection process (where is the prestige if all works submitted are shown?) or details which seem off (do you really need caviar and champagne at the private view, as promised by one open call 'art fair'?). Don't get suckered. There are sectors of the art world that make the catastrophically over-sold Fyre Festival look like a scout camp. If in doubt, ask around.

A good piece of advice which I shall pass along: fix yourself a budget for open calls at the start of the year and stick to it. This will focus your mind on the submissions that matter most to you and foster a sense of philosophical resignation rather than FOMO when your friends are selected for shows you did not apply to.

PRIZES

I have won three prizes in my life: one for a painting of an aeroplane when I was 8, one for a gingerbread family at a village fair when I was 13 and the last for a philosophy essay in my second year at university. Since then, zilch. Thirty-plus years, and the only prize our household has to show is my partner's 'Doggy Doppelganger' trophy for the owner most like their dog (hand on heart, a proud moment). It was only very, very recently that I realised you had to actually enter prizes for journalism and art critical writing to be considered. Yes, even the Pulitzer. I could have saved myself decades of bitterness.

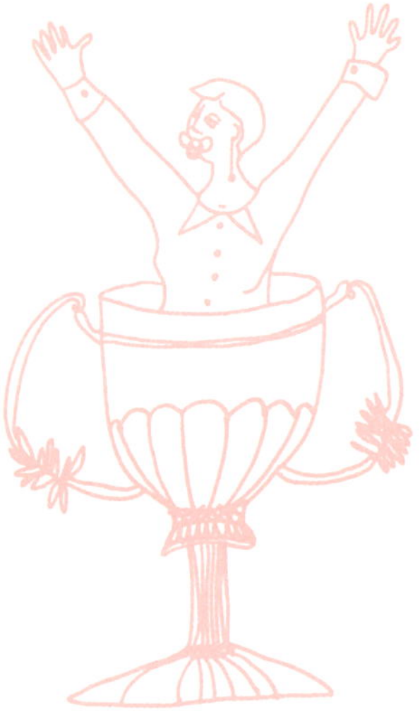

Things are different for artists. There are many prizes out there. Some you will automatically be entered for as part of an exhibition; others you will need to apply for. There are also awards for which you must be nominated by a third party. In most cases, there will be a cash prize for the winner. Some prizes will be in kind: art materials, mentoring, a residency or a solo exhibition. A few awards take the form of a commission.

Most open call exhibitions feature prizes, and all works accepted are automatically entered so long as they meet the criteria. The long-running Black Creativity Juried Art Exhibition hosted by the Griffin Museum in Chicago awards three Best in Show places with a separate category for under-18s, for example.

The process of entering for a prize is similar to applying for a grant or juried exhibition. Many are medium-specific. Read the small print and be honest with yourself about whether this prize is appropriate to the level you are working at. The Jameel Prize for contemporary art and design inspired by Islamic tradition is selected from open submission. A quick look over the standard of works short-listed in previous years makes it clear that only artists and designers working at a very elevated level stand a chance: in 2018, an architect won for the design of an entire mosque in Bangladesh.

Prizes by nomination come at every level, from the eminent MacArthur Fellowship – which comes with a no-strings-attached cash prize of $800,000 – to awards for emerging talent. Nominees are proposed by an invited jury composed of curators, writers, artists and other art world professionals. In other words, what all prizes by nomination have in common, no matter how humble, is that the artists most likely to be put forward are those who are getting themselves out there and making sure people are aware of their work.

RESIDENCIES

There are thousands of artist residencies – from isolated rural huts to gregarious urban studios – each functioning according to its own model. There are a few things to consider before applying, but if you can, you absolutely should. A residency takes you out of everyday routine and invites you to focus on your work for a fixed period. They can be particularly valuable for artists like you who are at a transitional point in their careers. A residency is an opportunity to experiment and take stock.

At its most basic, a residency is an invitation into a space for an agreed period of time. Almost all residencies will require you to actually be 'in residence' – in other words, they involve travel. The exceptions are studio residencies like those offered by the BINZ39 Foundation in Zürich, which awards local artists rent-free studio spaces for a fixed term.

Residency periods vary – from as little as two weeks to nine months or more – as does the level of provision. The most sought-after offer free accommodation and a free studio. Almost all will expect you to cover your travel to the residency and your food. They may offer specialist facilities such as a ceramic workshop, movement studio or darkroom. In some instances, there is an element of mentoring involved, or the possibility of interdisciplinary collaboration. If you are on a group residency, you will be expected to interact with the other artists, coming together over evening meals.

If you are on a fully supported residency, you may be expected to 'give back' by donating an artwork, presenting a performance or offering a workshop.

Most residencies are not fully funded and will expect you to contribute to your accommodation costs. Check the fees before applying – some residencies are run for profit and cost as much as a luxury holiday.

In *How Not to Exclude Artist Mothers (and other parents)*, I explored the difficulties parents faced when applying for residencies (among them, time constraints on the part of the artist and lack of flexibility on the part of the residency). I won't go back over the same ground here.[16] Things are starting to change, and more residencies will now accept artists travelling with a family. The Swiss arts council Pro Helvetia has an excellent international residency programme and has been notably proactive in accommodating artist mothers and other parents.

If you work full- or part-time, or are less free to travel, you may be able to find a two-week residency that could fit within an official holiday period. It may also be possible to divide a residency into chunks spread across a year. Many smaller rural residencies are run by artists, who tend to be more flexible and accommodating.

---

16 Hettie Judah, *How Not to Exclude Artist Mothers (and other parents)* (Lund Humphries, 2022).

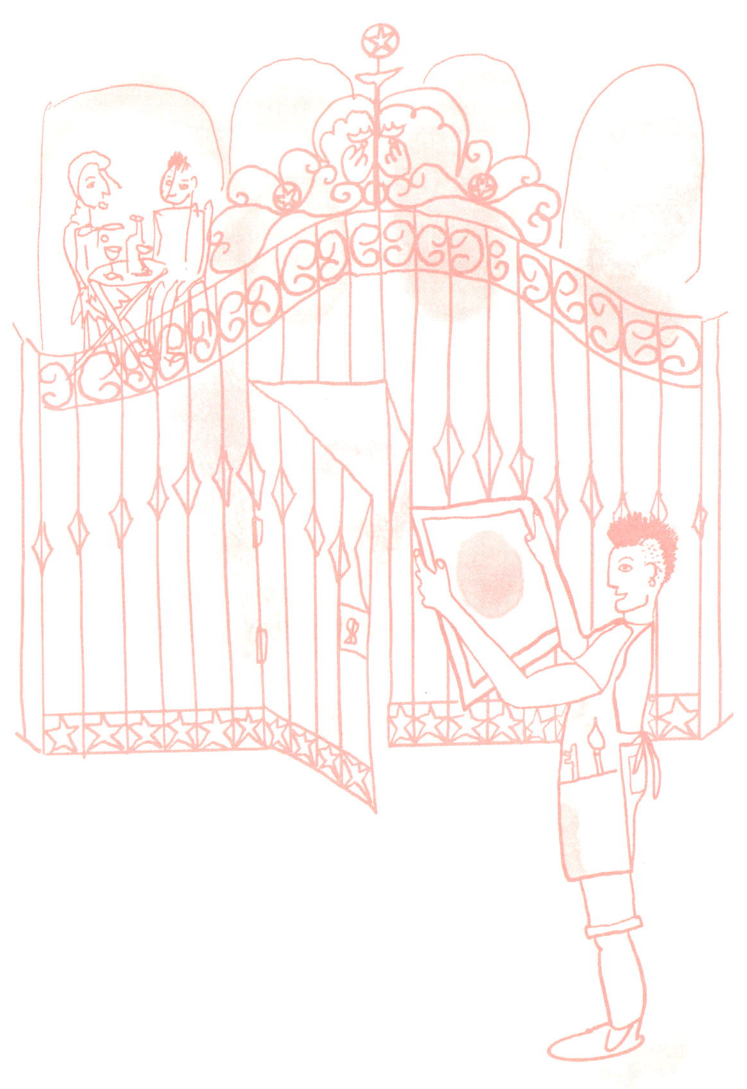

PART 6

SHOWING

You may have heard of Vivian Maier. How she was a New York City nanny who also happened to be a photographer of great invention and audacity. How she experimented with self-portraiture, was a delighted observer of human idiosyncrasy and revelled in the lush possibilities of colour film. Sometimes, she shot from a child's viewpoint, but Vivian the photographer led a parallel existence to Vivian the nanny. No one knew Vivian the photographer existed until her life's work – over 100,000 negatives – was found in a storage locker and auctioned for $400 a box in 2007. There has since been a documentary. A biography. Solo exhibitions in Europe and North America.

Vivian's story is considered heartwarming – the great artist who walked unnoticed because she was disguised as an unremarkable woman in domestic service. It is also tragic. Vivian never got to share her work, to see how it was received or to choose how it should be printed.

You may be a genius in the studio, but the world isn't going to come to you without good motive and an explicit invitation. No matter what you hope for, it is unlikely that you will achieve much if you don't make your work available for people to discover. The more you show it, the more likely it is that things will happen.

YOUR FIRST EXHIBITION
IN A LONG TIME / ever

Good news. You don't need to be invited to show your work: if you can secure art, a space and an audience, you can do it yourself. The strategies shared in Parts 3, 4 and 5 will have placed you in contact with fellow artists and creative people from your local scene. These, plus your family and non-art-world friends are, for your First Exhibition In A Long Time/ Ever, your audience.

The cheapest and most easily accessed exhibition space you have is your studio or, if you work from home, your home. You may have reservations about using your home.[17] They may be justified. Mine is neither a conducive environment for the contemplation of art nor in any danger of being photographed for an interior-design magazine. Also, my dog objects to sharing space with people having fun in company. Good for you if you have a chic, airy

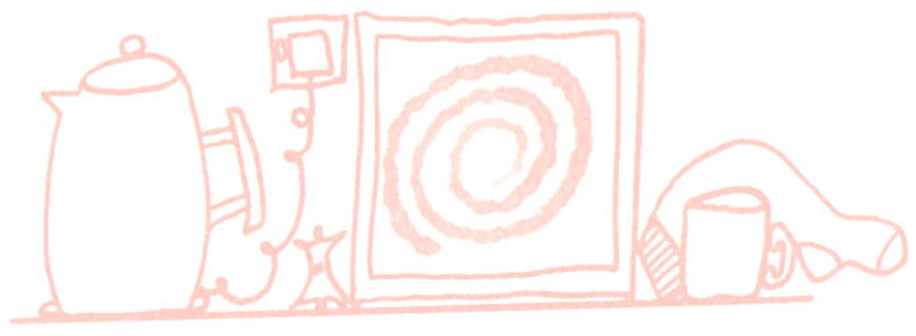

---

17   Some artist friends object to the cosy domestic associations of showing at home. 'I do not wish to exhibit my work,' hissed one, 'next to *cake*.'

dwelling and more tolerant canine companion. You can become part of an underground history of artists using their homes as exhibition spaces. My favourite is 42 Carlton Place, an occasional gallery on the ground floor of a terraced house in Glasgow, founded by the artists Carol Rhodes and Merlin James.

Whether using studio or home, the run of this exhibition should be short: one or two days is adequate. Invite people a month in advance. Remind them the week before. Make a digital flyer and post it on social media. Print off a list of works with prices and give it to everyone. Fancy art fairs and galleries do not show prices, but it's appropriate to do so in a studio exhibition. I assume forcing people to ask for prices is a way to filter out those who might worry they are unable to afford them. For the purposes of your First Exhibition In A Long Time/Ever, you should view everyone who turns up as a potential collector.

Your main outlay will be your time. If you start with an evening private view you might treat all the eminent collectors in attendance to beer or wine – or tea and biscuits if you hold a family-friendly mid-morning viewing instead.

For your Second Exhibition In A Long Time/Ever, you can astonish everyone by showing in a different space. (See how your career has progressed! Those who didn't invest at your debut show will be kicking themselves.) If your studio complex has a communal area, and (importantly) your fellow artists are amenable to your taking it over for a few days, this would be ideal. If you are now part of the community around your local arts venue, now is the moment to ask whether they'd consider hosting a show. Other free-to-use spaces might include a room at the local library, a community hall or an unused high street shop (n.b. – this last option will require both cleaning up and the permission of the landlord).

Do not turn your nose up. Such venues have been turned to magnificent and subversive ends by your predecessors. In 2020 Willesden Green Library exhibited late paintings by firebrand publisher and conceptual artist Rasheed Araeen. Artist and activist Monica Sjöö's *God Giving Birth* (1968) – now a mainstay of texts on feminist art – was first exhibited in St Ives Town Hall (then swiftly removed amid accusations of blasphemy). Who could mention exhibitions in empty shops without including Claes Oldenburg's cheeky New York show *The Store* (1961) – which he stocked with underwear, pie and pastries made of plaster – and Tracey Emin and Sarah Lucas's riotous east London enterprise *The Shop* (1993)? The joy of doing it yourself is that you make your own rules.

STAGING GROUP SHOWS

Depending on how fast you work and the quality control you impose on yourself (do, please, impose quality control), you are unlikely to have enough material for a solo show more than once a year, if that. More good news! In the in-betweens, you and other artists can stage group shows. If a couple of them are studio mates, then that communal space in your studio is a great place to start. If you are tempted by an empty shopfront or other disused space, it is MUCH more feasible to take it on as a group. You can share the cleaning duties and the invigilation. Staying late into the night to get the show hung will feel fun rather than mildly depressing. You can have an exhibition title. And a theme. You can even make a poster.

Some artists can be snotty about group shows, particularly as they get older. If you feel group shows are beneath you, or a waste of energy, there are good reasons to reconsider.

Showing as a group brings important benefits. Firstly, you can pool your skills, sharing the technical, social and administrative burdens of an exhibition. Secondly, you will massively expand your audience, each artist bringing their own network, friends and family. Five artists sharing a gallery will bring five times as many people into the private view, which means more eyes on everyone's work. Thirdly, sharing one another's work on social media opens up an even larger digital audience. This is one of the routes by which I find artists. Most gallerists and curators active on social media will look to artists attracting the attention and support of others, so such mutual support is crucial.

Group shows are also an opportunity to extend beyond your network. If there's an artist whose work you have admired from afar, approach them and ask if they'd like to be in a show. Most artists love being invited to show their work, and the likelihood is that they will say yes.

EXHIBITING AS A GROUP

Greater than the sum

If there are artists you enjoy showing with, why not formalise the relationship by declaring yourselves a group? I appreciate the ambition of those historic groups who named themselves like squads of superheroes (anyone else waiting for the Vorticists to enter the Marvel Cinematic Universe?). You can keep things simpler. If you have something in common you wish to shout about – ceramics, electronic music, dachshunds – let that inspire you. Otherwise grab a place name – if it was good enough for the Hudson River School, it's good enough for you.

Forming a group carries not unpleasing gravitas.

Congratulations, you've just written yourself into art history (just IMAGINE future PhD candidates poring over documentation of your first group show!). It suggests that you take yourselves seriously and wish to be taken seriously in return. No matter that, historically, most groups split after a few years due to abrasive personalities and messy sexual dynamics. For now, revel in what being in a group allows you to do. You can apply for exhibition funding. You can organise a public programme. You can contact press (at least a month ahead of the show, thank you), safely protected by the armour of the group.

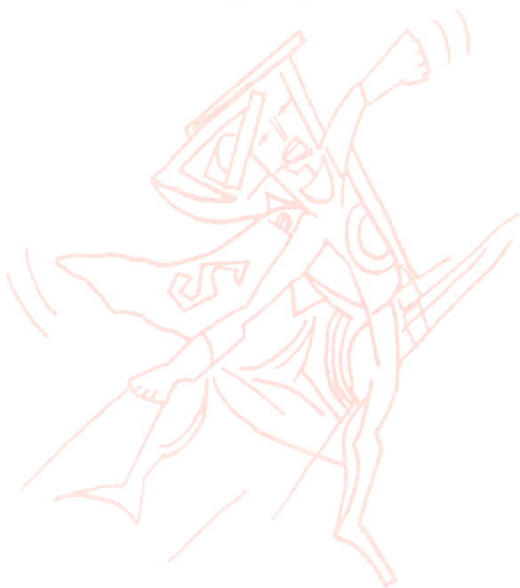

Many groups take the word 'collective' as part of their name. This is a little misleading, in that the group is not making work collectively – each has their individual practice as an artist. The collective action comes in pulling together for exhibitions and mutual support. One of the great strengths of a group is that you can, as one artist put it, 'borrow other peoples' personalities'. If you are an introvert, there will be group members who feel more comfortable taking a forward-facing role. The most numerate can run the budget. If problems arise, it tends to be because the division of labour has not been made explicit and one person feels they are shouldering an unfair amount.

The Mother Creatrix Collective was founded in 2022 by Shweta Bist, Kim Hopson and Jocelyn Russell, three artists living in the greater New York area. The collective has expanded to seven members, all of whom are caregivers to children and parents, and make art around the demands of salaried work and family life. As a collective, they organise one or two shows a year, hold crit sessions, skill-share and offer mutual support. They visit exhibitions together and are planning a group retreat. The structure is mutable and egalitarian, with labour apportioned according to capacity and with an understanding that the collective will pick up slack for members struggling with other demands.

What does forming a group offer? 'We feel more supported and confident as we move through the art universe,' say Mother Creatrix Collective. 'We have also been able to tap into each other's networks and expand our circle of outreach for larger support.' The group's activities have been informed by its members' diverse backgrounds and very different art practices, and shared experience as caregivers brings important empathy to crit sessions. 'We have formed lasting friendships that extend beyond our art careers. From the space of this small community we have built, we are able to reach out to other artists making important work around caregiving. It has been an enriching experience.'

ARTIST STATEMENTS AND EXHIBITION TEXTS

Back when I worked on the editorial team of *ArtReview* magazine, there was an evolving list of banned words taped to the wall – vocabulary that was modish, redundant or over-used. Novel words spread through the art world like scabies and are as tricky to eradicate. The source might be a briefly fashionable text, or a curatorial course, or an overabundance of artists entering psychoanalysis. Suddenly the same words are everywhere – everybody's art is apparently 'interrogating' this, or 'riffing off' that, or 'activating' something else. People and objects alike are praised for their 'generosity'. Some infestations are cutesy: 'critters', 'icky', 'thinginess'. Worst of all are grandiose academic borrowings. If you ever hear me shout 'for fuck's sake!' in a gallery, it's a fair guess that I've hit the word 'ontology' in an exhibition text.

Part of the reason that novel vocabulary circulates in this way is because a base level of insecurity afflicts almost everyone in the art world. When we read a text that sounds authoritative, it can be instinctive to borrow something from it to add to our own facade.

At some point in the process of sharing, exhibiting and publicising your work – whether solo, in group exhibitions or online – you will need to produce text to accompany it. The point of an artist statement or exhibition text is not to sound like a pompous academic who swallowed an advanced manual of psychoanalytic theory. The point of an artist statement or exhibition text is to invite people into your work. People who are not artists (and this includes even very prominent collectors) are often more comfortable in the world of words than the visual realm. Any text about art is, on some level, performing a translation between the two.

If you face writing tasks with horror, record yourself talking about the work with a friend or family member. Start by talking about what you were looking at, or listening to, or watching, or thinking about when you were making the work. Explain some of the ideas, as well as the technical process that went into it. Draw your friend's attention to small details. Listen back to the recording and pull out five strong points to use as the foundation of the text. Whether a personal statement or exhibition text, short is good – aim for one or two punchy paragraphs. Have a bookish friend check the text for grammar, punctuation and clarity.

GETTING IN TOUCH WITH CURATORS AND CRITICS

Barbarians at the gate

Gatekeepers. Another fashionable word in art circles. Gatekeepers decide whether you are permitted into the exalted realm of press coverage, curated shows and commercial representation. In other words, the principal art world gatekeepers are curators, gallerists and members of the media (old style and social). If you approach the gate to the exalted realm unheralded, the gatekeepers are unlikely to pay attention. If you have accumulated some combination of grants, awards, residencies and group shows, you will find yourself in a relatively attention-grabbing position.

Who to approach? I am regularly contacted by artists and curators asking for the email of [globally famous author of popular book on women artists] so that they can invite her to their shows. Firstly, I don't have [globally famous author of popular book on women artists]'s email – she works through a publicist. Secondly, I imagine [globally famous author of popular book on women artists] receives hundreds of exhibition invitations every day – more, by an astonishing degree, than it would be humanly possible for her to visit.

For the time being, forget trying to attract [globally famous author of popular book on women artists], ditto revered critics on national newspapers, international gallerists and the chief curator at the museum of modern art. Look instead to curators who have worked with people you know. Junior staffers at galleries you frequent. Writers on art magazines and newsletters you enjoy. Anyone following you on social media who you feel carries influence. Many of these people will have their email address or a contact form on their website. If not, send them a message to let them know that you'd like to email them info on an upcoming show. (You can make a first approach via DM, but do not send the actual info about the show this way – it will get lost almost immediately.)

Make your approach ahead of a group show. If it is an exhibition convened by your captivatingly named artist group, so much the better (gatekeepers like to feel in the loop, and a group that sounds like it's going places will intrigue them). Send a personal email about a month in advance. Address the gatekeeper by name and allude to something they have done recently (a podcast, exhibition or piece of writing you enjoyed). Everyone is susceptible to the flattery of attention. Keep your email very short – let them know about the show, include one or two enticing sentences about your work, and say that you would be delighted to make them a cup of tea if they visit. Do not anticipate or suggest more than this. All you want at this stage is for them to see the work.

If they don't respond, send a follow-up a week before the show opens. If they still don't respond, drop it. You can contact them again ahead of the next show, but more than two emails at this point will feel like harassment. If they do respond positively, try to arrange a time for them to visit when you (or the front-facing group member) can be there to walk them through. If they respond but have not visited by halfway through the show's run, send them a note reminding them of the closing date. Congratulations, you have started to nudge the gate open for yourself.

READYING A PROPOSAL

Outside of reality TV, you would not propose marriage to someone you didn't know. So it is with exhibitions. Any art centre or public gallery that you or your group approach should be well known to you. You should be a regular visitor and know the space, the programme and the people working there. All this will help you judge whether it is a good fit for your show.

If the person you are approaching knows who you are, they will be more responsive. If they do not know you, you should provide context – links to your website and recent exhibitions in your email signature, for example. Start with a simple email explaining that you're a regular visitor and enjoy their programme and would like to work on an exhibition with them. Would it be ok if you submitted a proposal?

If the initial answer is positive, it is best to present the actual proposal in person and talk them through it. You'll need a clear and comprehensible theme or concept for the show – something that can be expressed in a couple of sentences. Put together a presentation with images of works that you are hoping to include, and explain how these will be displayed in their gallery. If there is a built element or installation, show a mock-up of this in the space. Most art centres support specific community groups, so you might also suggest appropriate public programming. Be open to questions and suggestions. After your verbal presentation, you should send a proposal document containing the exhibition concept, artwork, installation images and supplementary information.

Don't be dismayed if it takes months to get a response. There will likely be fixed internal meetings over the course of the year at which future exhibitions are discussed. The art centre will need to contemplate their budget and their upcoming programme. Your proposal is likely to pass through many layers of personnel and bureaucracy before a decision is reached.

There are unpredictable reasons why an institution might not be open to a proposal – a planned construction project, a year of themed programming or a massive hole in their budget. They may also feel that your show isn't right for them. If your proposal isn't accepted, ask for feedback, and leave on good terms, letting them know that you would be interested in working together in the future.

ON PRESS

Much of what you need to know about press is covered above in the section on gatekeepers. In an ideal world, it should not be the artist's role to contact the press – it should be the gallery or art centre they are showing with. We do not inhabit an ideal world, and unfortunately artists often have to solicit press attention for their shows. (Do not solicit press attention unless you have a show coming up or a substantial project coming to fruition. Critics and art journalists don't just randomly write about artists. There always needs to be a notable event – in the media, this is known as a 'peg'.)

Professional press officers and PR companies will publicise an exhibition by sending out a press release – a one- or two-page document containing basic listing information (when, where, who), an enticing exhibition text, one or two images of work in the show and contact details. This is the information that you need to send out to any press you contact. You could put it into a press release yourself, though this is not mandatory.

Where professional press officers and PR companies (now sometimes known as 'cultural communications consultants') have a huge advantage is in their mailing lists and relationships with editors and journalists. An artist friend described the world of arts PR as a cabal, and she wasn't far wrong: these companies dominate the coverage in magazines, in newspapers and on social media. If you want to set yourself a really depressing exercise, buy all the art magazines ahead of the Venice Biennale and cross-reference the pavilions receiving the most preview coverage against the PR companies working with them: almost no pavilion without a big PR company will be getting much attention. These companies charge a lot, and for good reason, but it makes it tricky for anyone outside the cabal to get coverage. Don't try to beat them at their own game; there's no point trying to contact everyone – as above, a personal approach is always going to be most effective.

Your project may come with a bit of funding for press, but it is unlikely to be enough to pay for one of the big art PR companies. If you are wondering what to spend this funding on, my first question for you is this: what is it that you are looking for? Are you looking to publicise the show, or are you looking for someone to write an engaged response to your work? If it is publicity, then you might want to spend the budget contacting bloggers, influencers, young freelance writers and anyone whose writing, podcast and social media feed you enjoy and inviting them for a press day, for which you perhaps pay for travel, sandwiches and a cup of tea.

You can also try contacting critics. There is less critical writing published today than even a few years ago. Magazines have shrunk with the rise of social media, and even newspapers give far less space to art coverage, so you will have to present a compelling argument for why, of all the dozens of exhibitions opening that week, your show merits coverage.

If what you really wish for is a good piece of writing on your work, you might instead spend that budget on commissioning an exhibition text from a writer you like. (Be warned, however, that this text can't then be pitched for publication in a newspaper or magazine – art publications tend only to run material they have commissioned themselves.) Many writers enjoy this kind of work and will let you know quickly if they are up for it, so be ambitious in who you contact.

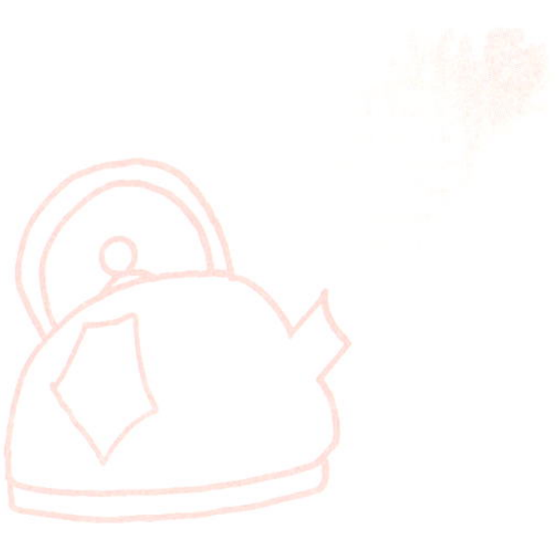

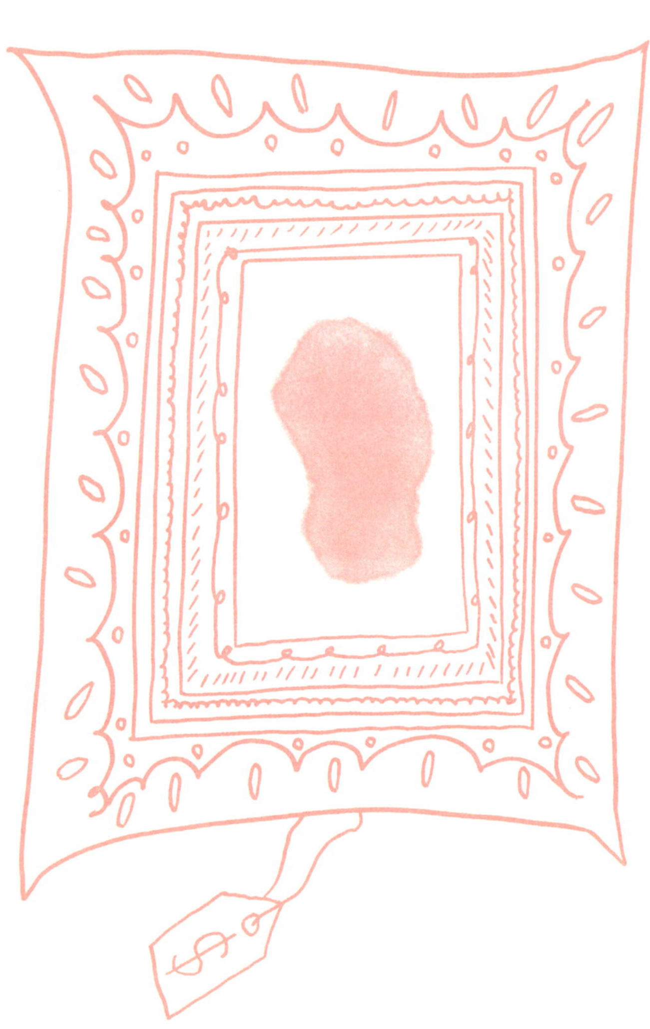

PART 7

THE SELL

Apparently you *can* put a price on it. Snobbery about selling your art is a hangover from the era of dissolute second sons slumming it as penniless bohemians. Not wanting to talk about money is for people who don't need to worry about money: refuse to put a price on your art or your time and you will be exploited. It's brutal out there. I would wish for all artists to be able to support themselves through their art, whatever it may involve. (Ok, perhaps not forgery. Or photorealism.)

The most evident route is representation by a commercial gallery. Many yearn for this. Gallery representation is a status marker – a hard-won sign of success, according to various metrics. It is not right for everyone. Nor is it the only route to selling work. (And selling work is not the only way to support yourself as an artist. We'll come to that in Part 8.)

Part 7 is a Frankenstein's monster of interviews with a dozen gallerists. Each has a different set-up. There's a recent graduate who started out showing his contemporaries, a senior figure in a blue-chip gallery[18] and another from a mega gallery with outposts on three continents. There

---

18 'Blue-chip' is a term the art market borrowed from the stock market to indicate investments that are well established and considered reliable. A blue-chip gallery is thus representing artists of global reputation with an established sales record. That the term has its origins in the world of poker arguably tells you everything you need to know about the illusory notion of a sure bet in any field.

are regional gallerists and metropolitan gallerists, gallerists entering the big time and gallerists who want out. For
candour's sake, I have kept identities secret. Their responses
have been aggregated and attributed to fictional characters:

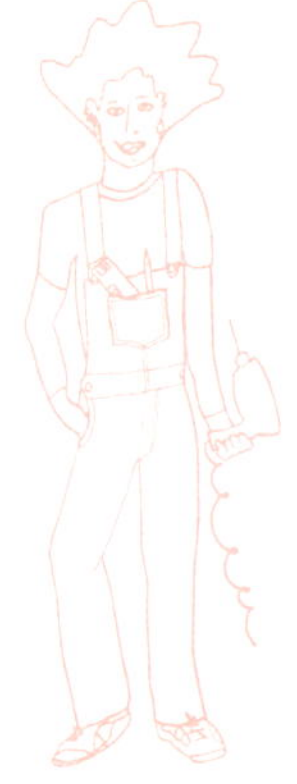

Young Gallerist

Recent graduate who opened an
exhibition space to show work by
their contemporaries. Young Gallerist
is a bundle of can-do DIY energy, and
takes care of everything, from painting
walls to chatting up collectors.

Solo Gallerist

Young Gallerist ten years down
the line, older and more cynical.
Still basically a one-person outfit,
supported by a revolving door of
poorly paid interns and technicians.
They have an amazing eye, know
everyone (and all the best gossip),
though years of having their star artists
pinched by blue-chip galleries has left
them jaded.

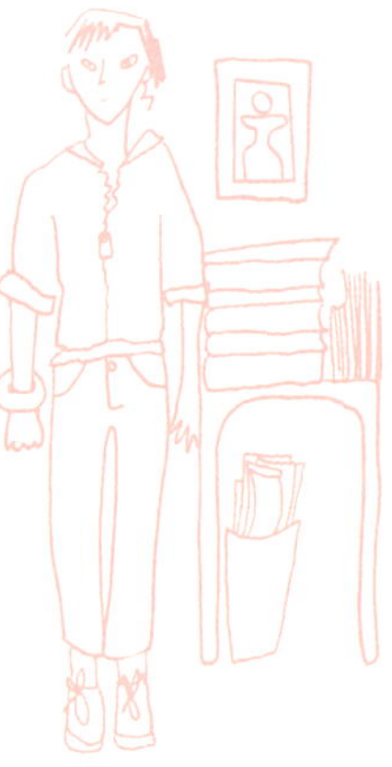

Mom & Pop Gallerists

Couple running an art gallery as a family business (mom & mom and pop & pop variations on the theme are also available). The gallery is a second career after unfulfilling success in another field, and they have entered it with considerable passion. Caring and involved, if lax in imposing boundaries between gallery and personal life. Have a gallery dog.

Regional Gallerist

Gallerist working beyond a major art-world capital – perhaps in a small town, perhaps in the countryside. The upsides: low rent and abundant space. The downsides: lower visibility and fewer passing millionaires. Regional Gallerist's mission is twofold: to develop a local market and to put on a dynamic programme to entice metropolitan collectors out of their geographical comfort zone.

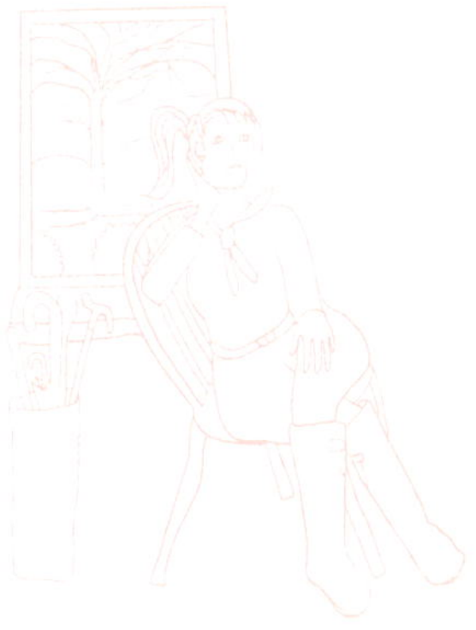

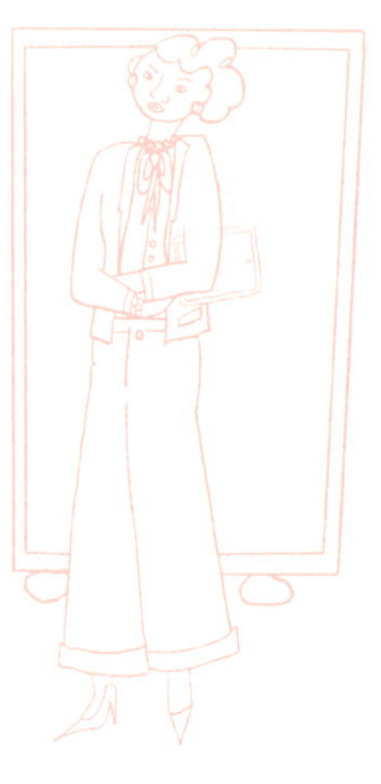

Blue-Chip Gallerist

Works for a well-established outfit with a substantial staff of artist liaisons and sales personnel. The stability of the blue-chip gallery is underpinned by a solid roster of star names and artists' estates, while their programme is spiced up by a smattering of younger talent.

International Gallerist

Positioned high up in a vast enterprise that stretches from Los Angeles to Hong Kong. Polyglot (a handful of European languages, plus Mandarin and/or Arabic), with the looks of an elegantly ageing Calvin Klein model, they exude an expensive ease that their wealthy clients find reassuring, albeit underpinned by permanent jetlag. The international gallery's roster is not dissimilar to that of a blue-chip gallery, it is just much, much larger (how else to fill 18 international gallery spaces and dozens of art fairs year-round?). Hoovers up artists' estates faster than nose candy in an art fair bathroom.

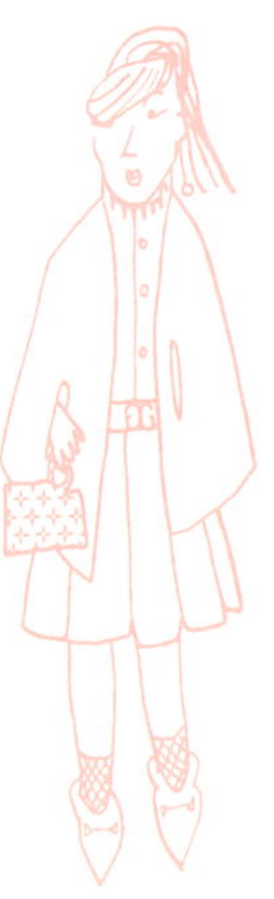

These fictional characters are not one-on-one representations of gallerists I have interviewed: each is an amalgamation of different people. This cast of experts will offer views into how commercial galleries work, how you might work with them, what the limits of the model are and why you might not – as Solo Gallerist puts it – want to know what happens behind the scenes in the sausage factory.

THE ECONOMICS OF THE ART GALLERY

Let us not be coy. Commercial galleries are shops. Some are high street. Others sell luxury goods, available not merely to the rich, but the right kind of rich. Like any shop, they have standard overheads: rent, rates, utilities, stock, staffing, advertising, marketing. They also have specific costs: art fairs, shipping, storage, photography and catalogue publishing. In pricing goods, they will need to factor in discounts, which will certainly be requested. They will anticipate peaks and troughs across a year, pay close attention to when these are likely to fall, and adjust their displays responsively. They will balance stock that allows them to appear edgy with more conservative fare they can sell.

To put that baldly, a gallery will need to turn over enough each year to keep going. To achieve that, it will need a core of bankable artists who produce enough work for regular shows and art fairs. Shows by the bankable artists will be timed for peak moments in the gallery calendar, when collectors are in town for an art fair or museum opening. The gallery roster will be fleshed out with artists who create exciting but less commercial work, and emerging artists (of whatever age) whose reputation the gallery is in the process of building. Some galleries also work with artists' estates. On the quiet, many also buy and sell works on the secondary market.

Nothing within this is predictable. The global art market has good years and bad. It is vulnerable to geopolitical turmoil, natural disasters, the stock market, elections, sanctions, freakish weather, economic jitters, fashions, scandals, vibes, whimsy and Mercury in retrograde (probably).

The gallery's top bankable artist might switch sleek metal sculptures for objects that resemble suppurating bones. The older woman artist they gave a first show to aged 65 might provoke a catfight among collectors. The hottest up-and-coming artist might show in a new territory and sell nothing, sending her nosediving into self-doubt. The air conditioning might pack up at the art fair, rendering it so hot that no collector will set foot, leaving the gallery with a vast return shipping bill.

Nothing brings this precarious balance more vividly into view than an art fair. The International Gallerist can suck up a few iffy art fairs. The Young Gallerist cannot. If participation in the fair costs £9,000 (and for Blue-Chip

Gallerist, they can cost ten times that),[19] and you add to that shipping, production, travel and hotels, then Young Gallerist needs to make £18,000 to break even. To do that they need to sell £36,000 worth of art over the five days of the fair, with 50 per cent of the sales price going to the artists. If gallerists look stressed to hell during art fairs, this is why.

The economics of running a commercial gallery are terrifying. You'd have to be mad. Or naive. The reason so many gallerists come from generational wealth is because they can afford to lose money.

(I write as the art market contorts itself through extravagant death throes like a medieval worm swallowing hot lead. I believe the technical term for this is 'a soft market'. If this were boom time, and senior directors were slurping beluga off interns' clavicles, I might be less sympathetic to the precarity and costs of running a gallery.)

COMMISSION

The other 50 per cent

The standard gallery commission is 50 per cent of sales. What does the artist get for this? At bare minimum, your work shown and people trying to sell it. A good gallery

---

19   This is a low estimate for an art fair fee. In 2018, *The Art Newspaper* made an informed guess that a stand at The Armory Show in New York would be between $10,000 and $100,000, with the average price being $40,000, Frieze New York would be $26,000 and Frieze London $24,300 (£18,500).

should do much more. They should closely manage your evolving career, focusing on sales to institutions and trusted collectors. If you are attracting some attention, they will try to ensure your work is not sold to anyone who might 'flip' it (sell it at auction for a profit). They will advocate on your behalf year-round, bringing your work to the attention of curators, art advisors and collectors.

Relationships between artists and smaller galleries can be intense and involved. The Young Gallerist, Solo Gallerist, and Mom & Pop Gallerists handle almost everything, from curating (and sometimes hanging) shows to writing exhibition texts to sales. You can phone them to chat through opportunities, forward emails to check if they are iffy (yes, that NFT offer is a scam), share new work, discuss ideas and confess your ambitions. It may have all the trappings of a great friendship, but it is not.

We love all the artists we work with.
We wouldn't be working with them if we
didn't enjoy hanging out with them. But
we're also conscious that the artists are not
our best friends – this is a transactional
business relationship.

Mom & Pop Gallerists

In a larger gallery, there will be salespeople, technicians, archivists, registrars, someone dealing with press, and liaisons appointed to artists as their point of contact. The artist liaison is part mentor, part administrator, part creative sounding board.

The liaison's responsibilities range from writing up contracts and checking legal issues to fielding telephone calls, assessing offers, weeding out time-wasters, overseeing press requests, supplying images for publication, checking clients' bona-fides and managing endless email chains with museums wibbling over possible shows. They are there in a crisis, or when you need to talk through your work, or feel like your head is exploding.

The artist liaison's most important job is
to free the artist and their studio from
distracting chores.

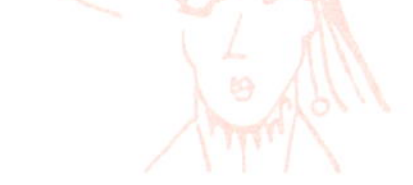

International Gallerist

Galleries support artists' participation in biennials and exhibitions. Awkward but true: few museums will stage an ambitious show without the support of a gallery. Depending on how big the gallery, and the artist, this might involve fronting the production cost of new work, and then discreetly selling said work.[20] Funding or partially funding exhibition catalogues. Paying for shipping. Loaning works from inventory. Next time you go to a monographic show, check for a gallery's name in the museum credits or courtesy lines. Yep, there it is.

FINDING THE RIGHT GALLERY

You have ambitions of representation, but which gallery? Finding a likely fit takes reconnaissance. Leave the house. Visit shows. Get a sense of the landscape. Forget about pressing the flesh at private views: actually go to see exhibitions and engage with galleries' programmes. Go to every gallery you've heard mentioned. Track down out-of-the-way venues. Find galleries that excite you. Think about what excites them in return. Imagine who their audience is, and what their collectors are into. Find galleries whose interests intersect with your own. Ones that champion women, perhaps, or working-class artists, or figurative painters, or printmakers.

If there are galleries you look forward to visiting, which hold public events you want to turn up for, put them on your list of galleries that might be a good fit. Becoming a regular visitor is the basis of any future relationship.

---

20 Though not all commercial galleries are discreet about this: some treat museum shows like particularly well-appointed showrooms.

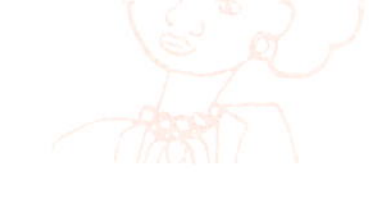

Blue-Chip Gallerist

Be realistic about where you sit in the ecosystem. Don't set your heart on the biggest, fanciest galleries. Look to those that represent artists you admire, who are where you'd like to be in five years. Galleries are notoriously guarded about prices, but with a little sleuthing you should be able to gauge their price range. Taking the gallery's cut into consideration, the bottom end of this range should not be a vast leap from what your work currently sells for. (Galleries are much more likely to be interested in artists who already sell work.)

The final reconnaissance stage is due diligence. Discreetly ask around. How does the gallery treat its artists? Do artists enjoy working with the team? Is the gallery organised and responsive? How have sales been? Does it appear to be in reasonable financial health?

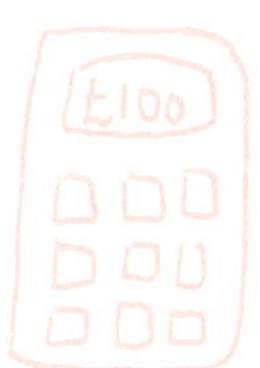

WHAT A GALLERIST IS
LOOKING FOR

Galleries have their own criteria in deciding whether to represent an artist. Some criteria are economic. All galleries represent artists at a range of price points, but that range varies gallery to gallery. Young Gallerist sells works priced between the low hundreds and the low thousands. International Gallerist has older artists selling in the millions but also wants artists selling in the tens and hundreds of thousands to appeal to a broader collector base. Blue-Chip Gallerist is interested in those whose works already sell in the region of £45,000 (often, they lure artists away from other galleries, or sign artists flourishing in another territory). Selling at this level puts considerable pressure on the artist to produce and deliver on sales, they admit: not all artists can face working like this.

Other top galleries are prepared to put time into building up an artist's market. They keep an eye trained on graduate shows and an ear cocked for buzz. International Gallerist represents a painter not long out of art school whose works sell for between £3,000 and £17,250. They signed her in the belief that they can push her prices much higher with a few diligent years of management and promotion.

When the market is struggling, gallerists tend conservative, looking to work judged easier to sell. What can be tricky to sell? New media, installations, photography, video and even sculpture. Prints, drawings and works on paper sell well but attract lower prices than oil paintings. Good news for painters, bad news for everyone else.

All galleries will consider how an artist might sit within their existing roster – whether they bring something new, while also fitting in. Will this artist appeal to their collectors? Will they be able to sell their works? A deciding factor will be whether they like and enjoy working with the artist.

> *The common factor in all the relationships*
> *I have with artists is that I like them as*
> *individuals. If I did not, my job would*
> *be unbearable.*

Regional Gallerist

Many artists ask how important a social media profile is in securing gallery representation, and I can understand their concern. As a writer, I am grotesquely jealous of the elevated prices paid to young, hot influencers for books of questionable literary or intellectual merit. It occurs to me that if I spent more time having aesthetic procedures and less in the British Library, my career would be more profitable. Publishing is very different to the art world: the business model depends on selling relatively inexpensive things to as many people as possible. If you have a huge following on social media, many will be able to afford a book. The business model in visual art depends on selling a small number of very expensive things and establishing a long-term market. You may have a million followers, but vanishingly few would be able to afford a painting from a blue-chip gallery.

Still, it's hard not to worry about all the buff young artists flexing on Instagram for a vast audience. Are gallerists salivating to sign them up? With a few caveats, no.[21]

I generally steer clear of artists who have risen fast through social media: I don't think they fit well into a traditional artist/gallerist relationship. Among other things, the celebrity and self-promotional acumen they bring into the relationship may lead them to believe they are doing all the work and don't require guidance or advice.

Blue-Chip Gallerist

---

21 Social media remains an important tool for getting eyes on your work – the distinction here is between those who use such platforms as a digital tool to promote their art and those who attract interest through their person or persona.

Those galleries interested in social media celebrities tend to work with artists short-term – one or two massively hyped shows, then on to the next overnight sensation. The only interviewee who judged social connections particularly important was Regional Gallerist. Being positioned outside a large city, celebrity clientele helps draw attention to the gallery, and a good local network can be translated into a pool of collectors who feel personally connected to the artist and the gallery.

CONNECTING WITH A GALLERY

No dating apps exist for artists looking to hook up with galleries. A shame, since the protocols are positively papal.

My first art job in the early 1990s was with a gallerist from Glasgow showing at the London Art Fair. As a student, I served wine and canapés at his private views. I had no experience bar my abilities with a corkscrew, but you need two people on an art fair booth otherwise you can't leave to attend to life's essentials. I was young and cheap, so there I was. I still remember the colour draining from his face as an artist approached with a portfolio of godawful drawings and settled in for a slow hour talking him through them.

Don't go up to a gallerist at an art fair to promote

your work – they are there to represent the artists on their roster. Solo Gallerist even gets anxious about close friends popping by the booth for a chat. Art fairs may look like social events, but for gallerists they are high-pressure work environments. Ditto private views. This is the gallery at its busiest, and everyone working there will be focused on the artist and collectors. If you want to build up a relationship with a gallery, do so slowly, visit the shows at quiet times, turn up for events, chat about the exhibitions. Once you have a conversational relationship, you can offer to add a gallerist to your mailing list (if you have one), let them know about shows that you are in and invite them for a studio visit.

Translating a friendly relationship into representation is not straightforward. As an artist, it is impossible to tell whether a gallerist is holding back because they are going through a decision-making process, because they don't think you are ready or because you are not the right fit. Most gallerists are friendly with many more artists than they will ever offer representation to, or even include in group shows. Blue-Chip Gallerist suggests that honesty is needed early on, so that the artist doesn't waste their time courting a gallery that won't take them on. I'm not sure this kind of upfront conversation ever happens in the awkward terrain of reality.

How the hell do artists and gallerists ever get together? Young Gallerist pays close attention to MA courses and graduate shows, working largely with artists of their own generation. They'll put them in a group exhibition or a solo try-out before committing to representation.

Most other gallerists depend on the collective intelligence of their network to turn up interesting artists: curators, collectors, writers and other artists on the roster. Solo Gallerist encountered one of their artists through judging an award. Regional Gallerist was alerted to an artist exhibiting in a studio show by one of their collectors. Mom & Pop Gallerists suggest that canny artists should focus on building relationships with independent curators. Curators often champion the work of artists they like.

We have junior staffers who keep tabs on independent shows and social media. Based on their suggestions, we put three painters into a summer group show and ended up signing two of them.

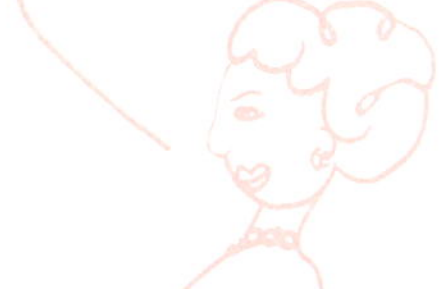

Blue-Chip Gallerist

Galleries use group shows in the less busy months as testing grounds. They might hire a curator, offering them a platform to work with artists who have attracted their attention. The gallery will gauge response to the show – whether the artists draw a crowd, whether their work sells (it is hard to sell from group shows), what the artists are like to work with.

The bottom line: to be discovered by a gallery, you must be discoverable. In other words, showing work. Studio visits are time-consuming, and tricky for Solo Gallerist and Mom & Pop Gallerists to schedule, since they have little time to step away from gallery duties. Most gallerists will want a discreet opportunity to see your work 'in the flesh' before committing to a studio visit. Embracing and creating opportunities to show your work will allow them to do so.

IF GALLERISTS DON'T
TAKE THE BAIT

You can do everything right, yet still nothing happens. Sometimes, it really isn't you. Or them. Among the reasons a gallerist might not take you on: the market is in free-fall and they're not taking on anyone. The style of your work is too similar to an artist they already represent. The subject matter of your work is too similar to an artist they already represent. You may see the gallery as a good fit, but the gallery does not reciprocate the sentiment. Your work doesn't currently sell for enough. You don't work at a scale or level of finish that suggests it will ever sell for much more. You work in a medium that they struggle to sell. You once slept with the partner of one of their collectors. You didn't wear your lucky underpants during the studio visit. You wore nothing but your lucky underpants during the studio visit. Your work is just... not their thing.

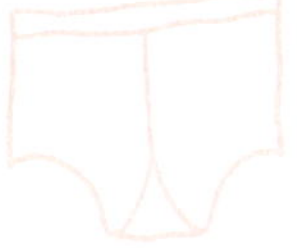

It stinks. It's heartbreaking. It can make you feel like quitting art. Please don't.

STARTING A RELATIONSHIP
WITH A GALLERY

A gallery is interested. What now? All being well, this is the start of a long-term relationship. Start as you wish to continue – generous-spirited, frank and mutually respectful. Discuss what is expected of both parties, and make sure you protect yourself. What should the gallery know about you, your life and your work? What do you want to ask them?

Few galleries issue contracts. You may consider this both dodgy and terrifying. I feel you would be right to. As things stand, it is the norm. Perhaps it will change. Mom & Pop Gallerists retort that a gallery that is going to shaft an artist will do so with or without a contract. A weasely view of things. More helpfully, Solo Gallerist points out that anything you agree with a gallerist in writing (email or paper) has some legal status.

What should the gallery be made aware of? Do you work very slowly? Let them know so that they can adjust their expectations. Do you have young children and prefer not to be contacted outside school hours? This should be easy to accommodate. Do you struggle with social interactions and worry about public events? This, too, should be discussed. It helps ease such conversations if you can offer workarounds: 'I can't be there for evening events but I'll happily answer questions over email.' 'I'm not great with big crowds, but I'd enjoy hosting collectors for studio visits.'

These conversations establish boundaries in your relationship. So long as you aren't shutting conversations down and refusing everything asked of you, they are useful for both parties.

Talk to the gallery about your aspirations and invite them to work with you in achieving them. You might want to collaborate with a choreographer or dream of a solo show in your hometown. There might be causes you wish to support through your exhibition sales.

What questions should you ask the gallery?

Money should be part of the conversation from the start.

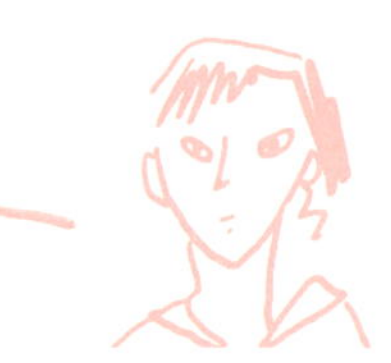

Solo Gallerist

No gallery should make you feel it is 'off' to discuss the financial aspects of the relationship. Ask them what their invoicing process is when works sell, and how long they take to pay. When preparing a show, ask whether they will offer key collectors a discount, and if so, what this is likely to be.

Clarify any agreement with the gallery about costs involved in producing or framing work. Some galleries will contribute to these costs, but you need to check the terms. Are they going to deduct costs after the sale of your work? The whole sum? Or 50 per cent?

When planning a show, agree a consignment period for the work.[22] When you consign your work to the gallery there should ALWAYS be an agreement drawn up specifying the period and outlining the terms under which you are consigning work to the gallery. A gallery will store consigned works that remain unsold after an exhibition and continue to try to sell them. Their inventory may be enormous. Galleries will keep their inventory 'working' for them by making it available for public exhibitions (I often borrow works from galleries for shows).

Having works consigned to the gallery saves artists from having to store them but puts you in a vulnerable position should anything go wrong. If the gallery goes bankrupt you may struggle to get work back. An artist I know spent years trying to reclaim her paintings after her gallery

---

22   The consignment period is the time that the gallery will hold onto your work and have the right to sell it on your behalf.

collapsed and eventually paid to transport them from Los Angeles to London.

Like your doomy thrice-divorced auntie, Mom & Pop Gallerists feel you should make sure that you are forewarned in case things go tits-up. What is the procedure if you wish to part company with the gallery? Is there a notice period? If so, how long? What if the gallery wishes to stop representing you? If there are unsold works in their inventory when you stop working together, when do you get them back? Who is responsible for transporting them to your studio? What happens if they are overseas?

WORKING WITH A GALLERY

There will be surprises involved, good, bad and simply unexpected. The gallery may relieve you of a lot of tedious admin work. They may offer constructive feedback on your work. You should be prepared for shows that don't sell – much or at all – and conversations about why this has happened. Does it worry the gallery, or not so much?

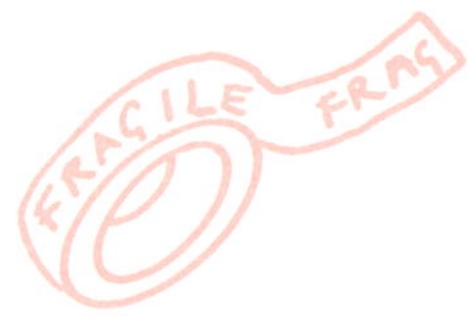

124

Solo Gallerist

Conservative pricing can lead to disappointment: an artist may have spent months working on something and wish to be better remunerated for their time. No gallerist will want to put themselves in the position of lowering an artist's prices, thus most with an eye on building a long-term market for an artist's work will err on the side of caution.

International Gallerist

Blue-Chip Gallerist describes the rhythm of working with a gallery. Ahead of an exhibition or art fair there will be great pressure on an artist to finish a body of work. Everything will feel urgent and communication with the gallery intense. This will be followed by a lull of months with very little contact. The artist will need to learn how to manage their time, and to spend the lulls quietly building up a new body of work or turning to other projects.

Regional Gallerist's relationships with artists are highly collaborative. The whole team want to discuss the work with the artist and hear about their ideas and processes. They want to work with artists who are generous-spirited and open to conversations about their work, not only with them but also with collectors and curators.

*We're not asking the artist to sell their
work, but we do want them to be able
to sell themselves.*

Regional Gallerist

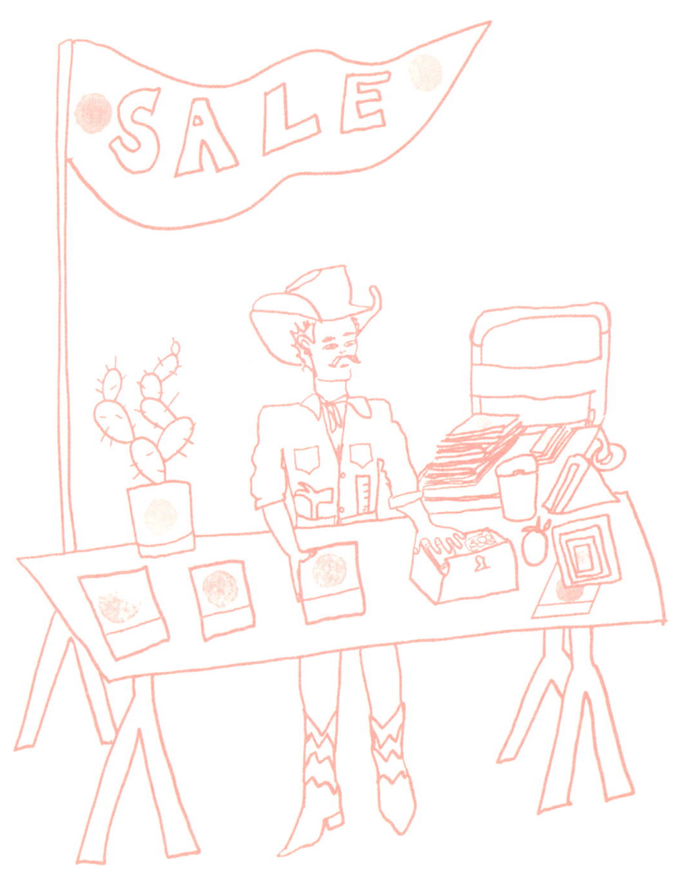
SALE

PART 8

A TRIP THROUGH THE MULTIVERSE

In the 1990s, Glasgow School of Art's most fashionable course was Environmental Art. It dealt more in atmospheres than objects: exciting, but hardly commercial. Glasgow had a dynamic art scene, but few sold work outside their extended circle. Exhibitions and art events were often organised collectively, in sympathetic institutions or disused buildings, sometimes supported by an arts council grant. Artists either took on paid work or signed on to unemployment benefit. With sales a negligible consideration, artists made and showed work with considerable freedom within the means available.

In the decades since, the understanding of what it is to be an artist has come to centre on the market. The expectation now is that the 'normal' state of affairs is representation by a commercial gallery. My gut instinct is that far, far fewer artists have gallery representation than otherwise. In other words, gallery representation is an exception to the norm, and most artists get by much as my contemporaries did all those decades ago in Glasgow, supporting themselves through grants, exhibition fees, salaried work and sales to friends.

Many artists actively choose against commercial representation. Perhaps their work is ill-suited to it, perhaps they prefer to manage their own commercial affairs, perhaps they find the more rabidly commercial manifestations of the art multiverse repellent. In Part 8 we explore other routes you might take, commercial or otherwise.

THE AGENT

The artist agent is a recent arrival in the art multiverse – I first heard the term in the mid-2010s. Each agent or agency has their own methods (the role is yet to become clearly defined). An agent is in some ways similar to a gallerist. They are public-facing, handle certain administrative matters, act as a sounding board and promote the artist – but there are crucial differences. Where the gallerist represents the interests of both artists and collectors, the agent works directly for the artist.[23]

The agent might manage sales of the artist's work but does not have a gallery, so they have fewer commercial overheads. While sales are a gallery's *raison d'être*, an agent might instead focus on public commissions, brand partnerships, legacy building, estate management or institutional

---

23   There are agent-type people who work with collectors – they are known as art advisors. You should probably add them to the list of gatekeepers to invite to your shows.

relationships. There are agents who specialise – in street art, surfer art, fantasy art. There are also agencies like HEKATE Studios that perform the role of project and studio managers, dealing with shipping, insurance, archiving, studio admin and production.

Inevitably, people on different sides of these relationships have different views on their advantages and shortcomings. Mark Segal started The Artists Agency in 2012 after years working in public arts organisations in the UK. Like a literary agent, Mark makes himself available to discuss ideas and projects with the artists he represents, advocates for them and makes connections on their behalf. He helps them write project proposals, appraises fee offers, checks their contracts and assists with funding bids. Eighty per cent of the work he does is in the public sector – his agency model is 'good for artists with less evidently commercial practice' – and his monthly agency newsletter is full of updates on collaborative projects, commissions and exhibitions.

The time I spend working with an artist varies enormously – I can spend a week talking to an artist every day, and then not hear from them in two months. When things are happening, there's a lot of talking things through. Artists are very sensitive – I sometimes help to draft emails, for instance,

Mark Segal, The Artists Agency

After testing different payment models, Mark settled on a flat annual subscription for which he's essentially on call. ('It buys you whatever you need, I don't count minutes,' he says.) For support over and above the norm – project management that involves budgeting, production and overseeing fabrication of work – he and the artist agree an additional fee, usually added to project budgets. He has never had to solicit or advertise – artists come to him by word of mouth.

The partnership between artist and agent is not always sunny. As with any close personal relationship, it can tip into dependency or acrimony. An artist – let's call him Emmanuel – contacted me privately to discuss his former agent (n.b. – not Mark). Emmanuel and his agent started working together when both were young – he became one of her first clients while he was still on his MA course. Their financial arrangement was commercial: she took a 30 per cent commission from sales she made or facilitated. She organised exhibitions and events for her artists at varied locations and promoted their work for inclusion in group shows at commercial galleries and art fairs.

At the time – in the early 2010s – most galleries had yet to grasp how to instrumentalise the digital realm.

In many ways, Emmanuel's agent was a classic disruptor. She created a strong social media presence, and made sure his work was properly documented and that he had a well-designed website. She was young and ambitious, and engaged with audiences and collectors of her generation. Emmanuel admits that the relationship was formative for him, but the fallout when it soured was catastrophic.

In part, this was a professional issue, because Emmanuel had depended on his agent for contracts and legal matters, and felt helpless and vulnerable when he was set adrift. But it also became a personal issue, because his agent had been his interface with the art world. Once things started to go wrong, she started to talk him down to the very people she had once promoted him to. In effect, it was much like a messy marriage breakup, leaving Emmanuel devastated and very wary.

What goes for agents goes for any professional relationship – do your due diligence and ask other artists about their experiences. Establish boundaries so that both you and the agent know what to expect from the outset. Make sure you have an exit plan.

SELLING YOUR OWN WORK

Selling art requires quite different skills to making it. You need to perform two jobs in parallel: creating artworks and running a commercial business. Direct sales are, by default, how many artists flog work, whether to friends and family, or through DIY and juried exhibitions, open studio events, fairs or digital platforms. You'll need technical competence ranging from bookkeeping to art packing. Above all, you will need to be organised and able to compartmentalise, so that you allocate dedicated studio time as well as set periods for desk and sales work.

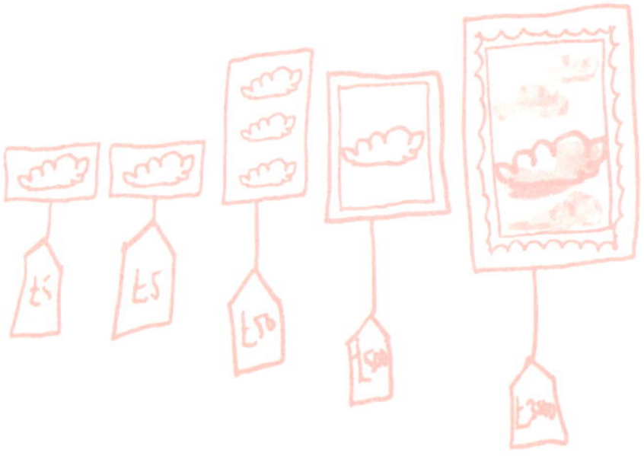

The practice of pricing art is quasi-occult. There are formulae that generate prices by the square centimetre or by adding material and labour costs. Oh, that things were so simple in the real world! Value is attributed to artworks according to variables including an artist's sales record, exhibition history, prizes, presence in notable collections, gossip, hype and buzz. There is a hierarchy of media: oil paintings are generally valued above drawings, while multiples and editions are priced lower than unique works. Get a sense of how your peers price work (n.b. – work that has actually sold) as a point of comparison. No matter how devoutly you believe rich people are idiots, do not wing it and price your work as if for gazillionaires: having to lower the price again will not instil trust in prospective collectors. Once you have settled on a realistic price, stick by it with confidence: this is the value you are placing on your ideas, your experience and your hard work, and you should never feel the need to apologise for that. (Decide in advance whether you wish to offer discounts to favoured collectors, as a gallery would.)

The guidelines to DIY exhibitions in Part 6 (p.86) cover some of the basics for direct sales. Other routes may also serve you well. There are specialist fairs for prints, graphic art, ceramics and photography, and big tent events such as The Other Art Fair and Affordable Art Fair. Unlike Frieze and Art Basel, most specialist and affordable fairs accept applications directly from artists. Admission for most is selective – you will need to apply – and the cost of participation will vary according to the space you need. Fees for the 2025 Hepworth Wakefield Print Fair ran from £200 for a table to £400 for a booth, for example.

The good news: these fairs attract a ready audience, there to buy art. By contrast, many people (ok, perhaps just me) attend Frieze mainly for the plastic surgery fails. The bad news: not all fairs are successful – it's a crowded market. Visit one before applying and ask artists how sales have been. Adopt your entrepreneurial persona to assess the fee. This is a work expense: does it provide value for money? As with juried exhibitions, some fairs overcharge and underdeliver. If the fee is suspiciously high, or the fair doesn't have an established record, proceed with exceeding caution.

Fairs are hard work, physically and mentally. You need to transport the art, unload and display it, be on your booth throughout opening hours and prime your chat to engage with punters. (Tell potential collectors stories about your art that they can go on to recount once they own it.)

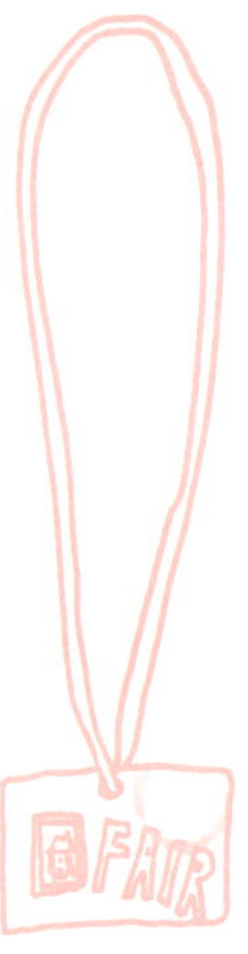

Essentially you need to be the staff of a commercial gallery – art handler, technician, curator and sales team – in addition to the artist. For logistical reasons (how to eat a sandwich? Or buy coffee? Or pee?), it helps to split a booth with another artist. If you are personable and enjoy talking about your work, fairs can be a fantastic platform, not only for selling but also for establishing relationships with collectors who might make a purchase down the line.

ONLINE MARKETPLACES

The digital landscape changes so fast that covering it in the stately medium of print seems quaintly doomed. Until around 2023, makers, craftspeople and artists producing affordable work with broad appeal achieved decent sales through platforms like Etsy. This has since become challenging: there are more sellers, fees have increased, the algorithm is harder to game and sites are flooded with AI-generated images.

A surprising number of artists now find sales through Instagram, either as a direct sales platform or as a route to solicit enquiries and direct people to a website.

Dedicated online art sales platforms are becoming sophisticated and sell work at surprisingly elevated prices. (Yes, people will spend thousands on a painting they've only seen on a tiny screen. I know.) Many art sales apps are optimised for viewing on a phone, creating an interface much like Instagram in which everything is for sale. They have curated selections, art advisors, online exhibitions, themed strands and other stimuli to keep collectors checking back.

Most platforms support themselves through commission on sales (Saatchi Art takes 40 per cent); some also charge a fee (Gertrude charges £20 to join, a monthly listing fee of £15 and 30 per cent on sales). They offer a dynamic and enticing interface for collectors to discover artists, follow their careers and acquire work, as well as attractive perks such as affordable mentoring or sales advice, but they are essentially business tools. You will still need to manage inventory, take and upload high-quality images, and market yourself and your work to generate sales.

PRIVATE COMMISSIONS

Private commissions require patience, diplomacy and a thick hide. Whether a mural, a painting reworked to match someone's decor or a portrait, whoever commissions it will likely have OPINIONS and feel entitled to share them. For this, among other reasons, private commissions are more demanding and time-consuming than self-directed work. Set your prices accordingly.

Everything thus far about getting eyes on your work, publicising and marketing it pertains likewise to private commissions – the key difference is that on all platforms and at all events you should clearly advertise this aspect of your practice. Attracting clients will be easier if you specialise. Your niche might be *trompe l'oeil*, saucy caricatures, nursery decor or stately portraits: signal this clearly and consistently to help people find you. Of course, most artists do all kinds of things. The popular canine portraitist Sally Muir also paints people, landscapes and dead baby birds, but it's the dogs that pull in the clients, and it is they for which she is known.

In drawing up an agreement, clearly outline what you will need, what you will provide and how the costs break down. Take into consideration the consultation period and your travel and materials, as well as your time. Allow for contingencies (specifically, the client asking for adjustments or revisions). Do not undersell yourself – you need to be consistent in what you charge. If you are unsure about your fee, imagine yourself invoicing that same amount for every job over the next two years. Is that sustainable?

Present a realistic timetable for completion and delivery. If your commission is for a portrait (human or animal), specify whether you will be working from photographs or from life. If you will be working from life, detail the number of sittings and their duration and frequency. Will they be in your studio, or at a location significant to the sitter? Outline what these sittings involve so that everyone is well prepared and comfortable.

As with direct sales, you are working two jobs here – artist and entrepreneur. One important distinction: your main goal is not the initial sale (securing the commission), but word of mouth once it has been fulfilled. No one sells your work better than a satisfied customer, and since people tend to socialise in cliques (dog-lovers, young parents, landed gentry, lavish decorators…), their social network will be an important source of future commissions. Truly, charm and knowing when to bite your tongue are your great assets.

PUBLIC COMMISSIONS

Public commissions range in scale from performances to permanent structures. Many are allotted through an open call and a multi-tiered selection process – from those who entered, a shortlist of artists is invited to submit a more detailed proposal, perhaps including a maquette.

Putting together a proposal is time-consuming. It must be specific, responding to technical challenges and cultural context (which you should research), as well as the brief. The jury will expect you to explain and defend your proposed work, provide an accurate budget and timeline for realising it, and have considered its resilience to weather, pigeons, graffiti, drunks, dog pee and small children. Big commissions require appropriate experience. For example, proposals for the UK's LGBT+ Armed Forces Community Memorial were solicited from artists 'with previous experience of public sculpture' and 'a previous commission to the value of £50,000 or more'.

All this palaver is draining for those who make it to the shortlist but not beyond, but as with all awards, once you get one commission, chances improve for subsequent proposals. Within the art multiverse, there are worlds in which public commissions represent a significant income stream because the state mandates spending on art as part

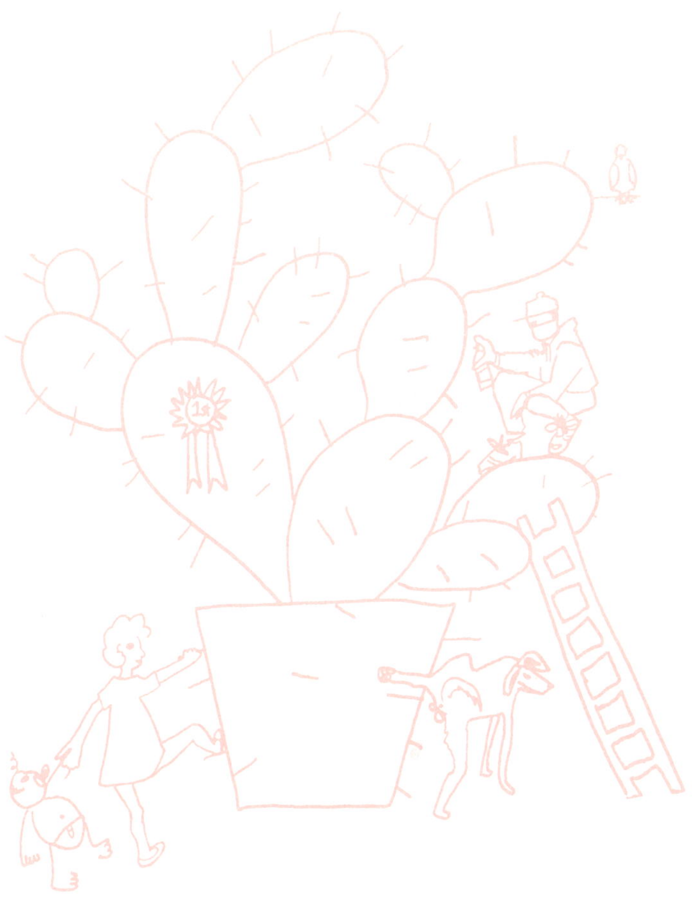

of building and development projects. In Denmark, 1.5 per cent of the labour costs of all larger state construction projects is allocated for art, which might include light and sound works as well as sculpture and painting. In Sweden, most regions and municipalities likewise apply a 'One Per-cent Rule'. Ireland has had a similar scheme since 1978.

There are potentially many years between the sub-mission of a proposal and its realisation. Along the way you will need to navigate entangled bureaucracy, the demands of competing local interests and omnidirectional feedback that feels like being stuck in the group chat from hell. At the end of it, however, you'll have created something enriching that will be experienced by a potentially huge audience.

The complex demands involved in applying for and realising public commissions (sculpture in particular) have historically favoured certain types of artist over others – those with a large studio set-up, assistants and the space to work at scale. A collective of artist mothers I worked with in Sweden complained that commissions invariably went to male artists with substantial existing support. The lack of diversity within public commissions is now widely recog-nised, and initiatives have been established to address it. In the UK, these include the Royal Society of Sculptors' First Plinth Award, intended as a springboard commission for artists interested in working in the public sphere.

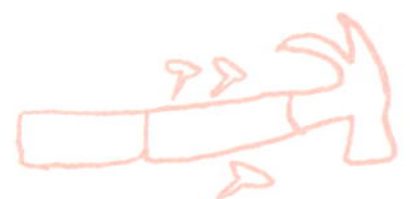

Cake is the currency!

Art can perform as a magic cloak beneath which social conventions no longer apply. In the name of art, you can invite people to participate in grand rituals or eccentric ceremonies, to suspend disbelief and antagonisms. Jeremy Deller has used the magic cloak of art to restage a clash between striking miners and the police, create an inflatable bouncy replica of Stonehenge and populate train stations across the country with soldiers in First World War uniforms. Jeremy is one of the best-known artists in the UK. Much of what he does is 'social practice' – public art that exists as events and encounters rather than lasting objects. He is commissioned by and collaborates with art institutions, but generally works beyond their walls.

Social practice has real-world impact. Suzanne Lacy, a pioneer in the field, has led projects that engage with sexual violence (*Three Weeks in May*, 1977), police brutality and social justice (*The Oakland Projects*, 1991–2001) and sex work (*Prostitution Notes*, 1974). Even when Suzanne's work calls for change in legislation and public behaviour, she approaches her subjects in creative and unconventional ways. As part of *The Oakland Projects*, she worked with local youth for two years to stage *The Roof is On Fire*, a filmed performance during which 200 young people sat in parked cars discussing race, gender, inequality and other issues on which their opinions were seldom heard.

No doubt there are art school courses on social practice these days, but none of the artists I have worked with studied it. Indeed, artists seem to be led to social practice by vocation rather than training.

It took Tereza Bušková two years to get onto an MA at London's Royal College of Art, but she persisted. Her work with communities came out of an experience navigating cultural sensitivities while making a film in Moravia in the Czech Republic. Each of her public projects in the UK has faced an upset – for one she had to repay grant funding, for another she lost the venue at the last minute. Across many rounds of rejected grant applications, she has taken on feedback, made adjustment and resubmitted, until the application is successful. She has what Brits call 'vim' and Americans 'moxie'.

Tereza creates lyrical social magic through public projects that bring together multi-national folk traditions and diverse local groups. In 2016, she led her community in the UK city of Birmingham in the ritual *Clipping the Church*, during which they encircled a place of worship through the simple intimacy of holding hands. Derived from an ancient English custom of the same name, *Clipping the Church* brought together people of diverse heritage and differing political affiliations ahead of the Brexit vote. It was the result of achingly long preparation. Tereza applied for funding with a young curator who offered her an institutional partnership for the project. She conducted workshops with a hospice, with Czech and Slovak communities and with a primary school. She solicited support from the local police, who suspended traffic for the procession.

The spectacle was ravishing, with folk costumes, embroidery and the knotted decorative loaves that have become a feature of Tereza's work. She has since gone on to lead projects with mothers from immigrant communities and survivors of sexual violence. All have required slow groundwork, she explains: 'You can't enforce community spirit: you have to grow it organically.'

What equips you for social practice? Willingness to work slowly and be flexible, says Tereza. Ease with people. Tenacity. Vision. 'Things happened by creating contacts and giving something in return – I might give an artwork or a loaf of bread. Over the years I have developed strong relationships and bonds, not only with organisations but with other artists I work with. If there isn't money, I bake them a cake. Cake is the currency!'

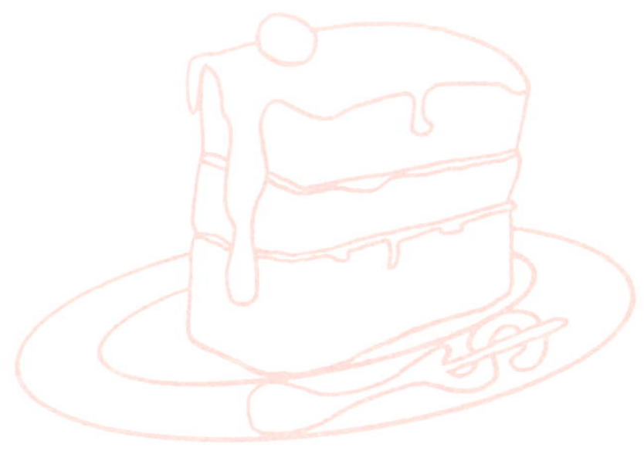

I spoke to the interdisciplinary artist Abbas Zahedi while he was installing a public project for London's Tate Modern. Like Tereza, Abbas is institutionally bilingual – fluent in both the language of art institutions and that of corporate and social organisations. He's initiated projects with a community centre, a food bank and a soda manufacturer. During the pandemic, he created a sound installation that functioned as a support space for health workers (this was serious stuff – Abbas's report on *The Sonic Support Group* was presented at a neurology conference).

He has an ongoing working relationship with healthcare providers and feels that art can play a major role in wellbeing. Not in a naff 'come be healed by Van Gogh' sense, but in inviting people to experience or consider the world in different ways. Specifically, giving the permission to think creatively in an arena (such as medicine) where that might otherwise be frowned on. His role is often to ask: 'What is it that art can do that other things can't?' He makes a crucial distinction: he's not a service provider. What he does is not art therapy. It takes time for trust and ideas to emerge and a project to take shape: 'Often the things I'm doing have meandering trajectories before they come together in a more meaningful way.'

Social practice is hard work. There is a very real risk of burnout. To work like this in the long term, you need an honest understanding of your own capacity, to delegate and collaborate and, perhaps most importantly, to know when to ask for help.

WORKING AS A COLLECTIVE

Many of the challenges and issues discussed in Part 8 – the need to divide energy between different roles, learn on the job, manage your capacity – are greatly alleviated by working as a collective. As a collective, you can become a reciprocal sounding board, benefit from one another's know-how, divide the cost of an art fair booth, put together proposals and pick up the slack when there's a personal crisis. When things go awry with agents and gallerists, those artists who are most dependent on those relationships are also the most vulnerable. As a collective you have the resilience of diverse perspectives, as well as skills that might include appraising a contract, putting together a project budget or – crucially, it transpires – baking.

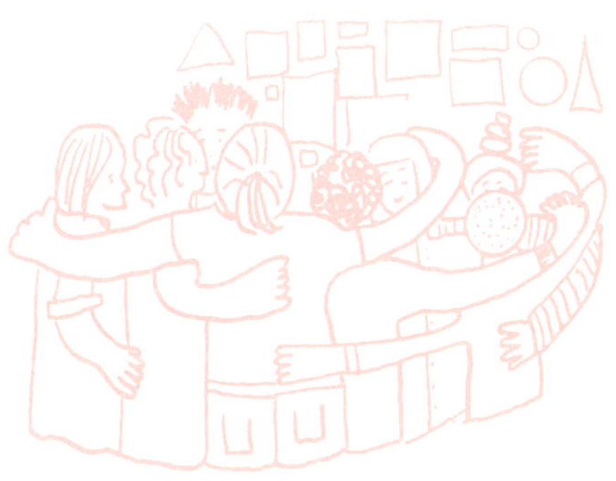

FANTASY

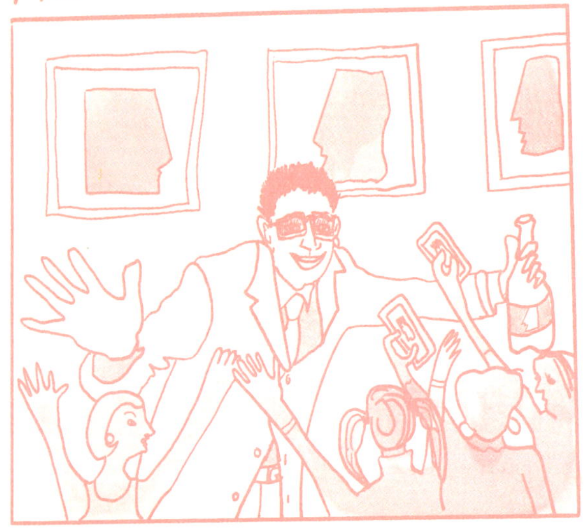

REALITY

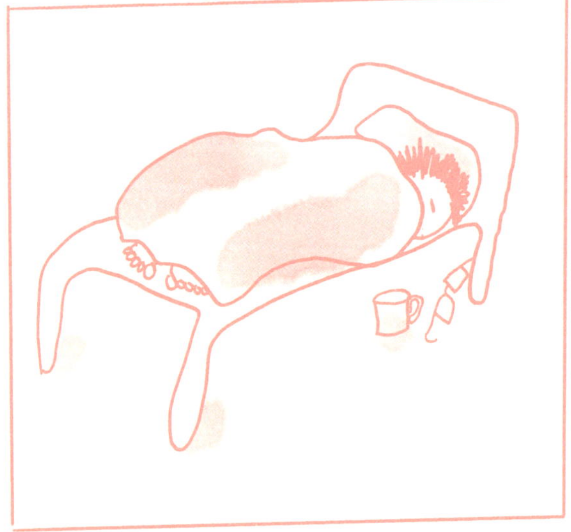

PART 9

MISFITS AMONG MISFITS

Career advice doled out to artists tends to favour those who are extroverted, charismatic and socially adept. It advocates strategies borrowed from competitive corporate environments (which, fair enough, some art worlds are). Artists are exhorted to network, to develop their personal brand, to adopt active sales strategies and to market themselves avidly. The trouble is that very few artists take naturally to such upfront behaviour, and many are actively terrified by it. A significant proportion of artists identify themselves as shy, introverted or neurodivergent. This habitat is a harsh one for wallflowers.

This is a misfit chapter. It is the result of correspondence with over 50 artists from around the world about their experiences of – and coping strategies for – situations that feel forbidding, overwhelming and even unkind. Although these interviews are anonymous, I wanted everyone to express themselves in their own words, so in this chapter I come to you as one voice among many – part of a Misfit Chorus. Sometimes the voices within the Misfit Chorus agree with one another, and sometimes they do not. So it is with misfits.

The Misfit Chorus reminds us:

*Since the beginning of time, our greatest artists
have been odd, awkward and often introverted.
Most of the brightest artists are unlikely to be
the life of the party at a social event. They're
often friendly and incredibly interesting but you
have to crack them open, gently, with patience
and understanding.*

I worry about an art world that rewards charismatic extroversion above all other qualities in an artist. I think such a world is in great danger of losing sight of what is most interesting in art. All being fair, it would be the job of collectors, curators and others to better accommodate artists. For now, we need alternative strategies and perspectives on how to navigate this business, interact with people, express needs, establish boundaries and stop your head exploding.

EXHIBITION OPENINGS

The term 'private view' can be a misnomer. You might imagine a hushed event animated by the crackle of champagne on glass and delicate crunch of canapé under foot. In truth, you are more likely to find your face crushed into somebody's Sandqvist backpack in a stairwell scented with spilled beer and the waft of watermelon vapes from the pavement below. Far from being private, the launch is invariably the busiest moment in an exhibition's run, and the one time you might struggle to actually see art in a gallery. It is important to turn up and support artists (and other art world people) you know. The private view of an exhibition is a big deal. They may be nervous. Friendly faces will mean a lot, even if your friend is too caught up to speak to you in the moment.

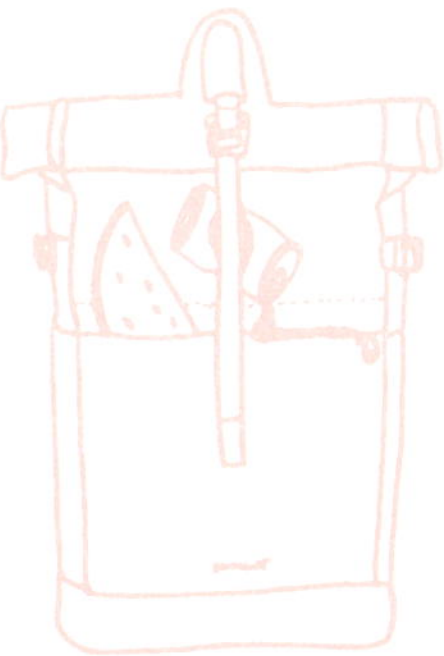

It's not just a hunger for culture that drives arty types to exhibition launches. Nor is it the free IPA. In the push to turn artists into entrepreneurs, collateral damage has been done to the private view. Artists and other art professionals have been fed the idea that these events are their prime opportunity to network, and that they should attend as many as possible so that they can meet important people on the scene and make themselves known to gallerists.

I think delicacy is in order here. There's something distinctly off about treating another artist's exhibition launch as your own networking opportunity. Turning up to someone else's show with the intention of promoting your own work is akin to turning up to a wedding dressed as the bride. By all means go to private views looking for an opportunity to chat about the art on show (for this, too, is networking). If the person you want to talk to is the person running the gallery, then this is not the time to introduce yourself, or to start talking about your own work. Their attention will (rightly) be on the artists in the show, and the collectors and curators they hope to interest in their work.

If you loathe private views (as I do), don't go unless there's someone specific you want to support. There are easier ways to be an engaged part of your art ecosystem. I often spend a Saturday afternoon going around clusters of galleries. As well as being able to see the art, it's a quieter time to chat to other visitors, or the gallery staff. Write in the visitor book. Share images of works you like on social media. If you really like the show, send the artist an appreciative message. Many commercial galleries host talks related to their exhibition programme – these are a great way to engage with the gallery and its artists in a more structured way.

I've noticed people will attempt to network with you when you are well dressed. If you look a bit scruffy, they're not interested in conversing with you.

*Be generous, introduce people,
open out conversations.*

*If I didn't manage to greet someone
I care about at an opening, never
mind. I can fix it by writing an email
instead of letting guilt eat me up.*

*I make it a game. I'm allowed to leave a
private view after I say hello to two
people I've not met before. This also
works well as a game with an artist friend
you feel you can be vulnerable with. You
both have to say hello to one new person,
and then you introduce that person to
each other.*

*My best coping mechanism is that I must
talk to one person before I can leave an
art event. One person and then I am gone!
As a result, I am careful and intentional
with who I do talk to and sometimes
it's forced me to meet great people.*

*If I have advice, it's to not talk
about your work. Talk about
the gallery and the show.*

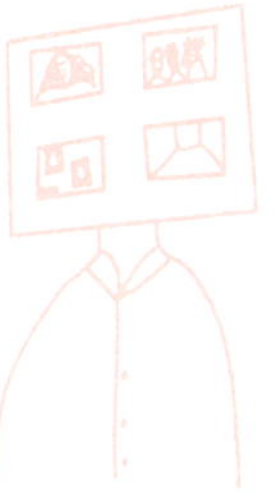

Going with a group of friends is not so helpful, because you end up hanging out together instead of meeting new people.

Be the friendly-looking person at other people's exhibitions.

I try to find art events that have organised talks attached so there's something immediately on hand to engage with and talk to fellow participants about.

YOUR EXHIBITION OPENINGS

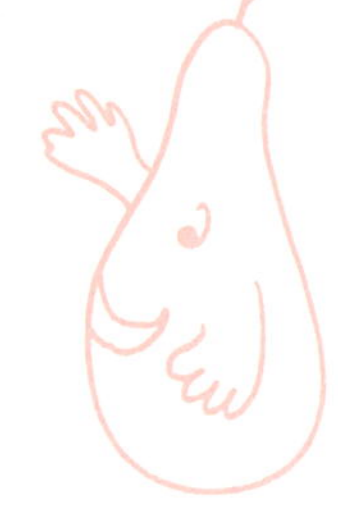

While you can get by quite well without going to the launches of other people's exhibitions, wriggling out of your own is a stickier proposition. Of course, it's not mandatory. Both Tala Madani – famous for her *Shit Moms* paintings – and the conceptual artist Ghislaine Leung sometimes don't turn up to the openings of their own shows, but they are artists with young children who are showing internationally with multiple exhibitions a year. As an artist who is just starting to show (again), each exhibition is an important marker. Having strategies that might help you celebrate and even

154

enjoy the occasion is important. Since the private view is a celebration of you and your work, you can choose to create the atmosphere that works best for you. It doesn't need to be an evening event with alcohol: it could be at 11am on a Saturday with tea and pastries. You can make it child-friendly. You can programme a structured event such as a workshop. You can bring props for yourself – sketchbooks or maquettes – so that you have something to do with your hands.

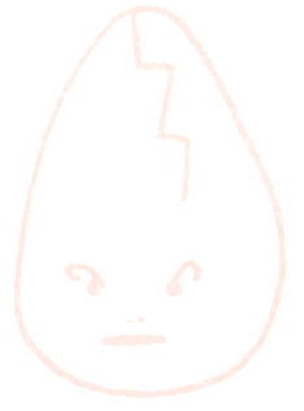

When it comes to promoting my own work, I find it exhausting. If I have a role (such as running a workshop or giving a talk), I can do that successfully.

I am the artist that I am because I am introverted, sensitive, feel and think deeply and enjoy solitude. I am so tempted to hide my work away and never have to show it to anyone, but it is as if I am being called to face my fears and get my work out there. I wish it didn't have to involve openings and networking though! I wish I could just show my work without having to be a face for it. I would consider asking if any opening event I have in the future could be scheduled for the daytime to make it easier for me to attend with my children.

*I find social settings much easier
to navigate when the setting feels
safe and there is a clear structure
(or where I have a task).*

*Arrive early so as not to have to embrace
a whole room full of people. Feeling
awkward is ok and doesn't last: the first
friendly eye contact is enough to break
the awkward spell. Talk to one person
at a time. Start with 'hello' and ask
them questions; make it about them.*

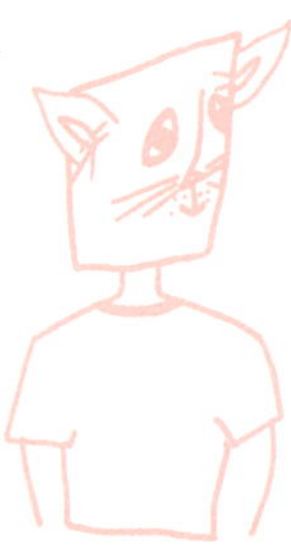

*Early on, I was so intimidated that
I started to use a very simple trick.
I intentionally became my 'dog self'
during events and then retreated to my
normal 'cat self' afterwards. As silly as
it may sound, it helps me to visualise
and adopt a more confident mindset.*

*I bring my loom to shows as much as I
can. People love to see how the work is
made, but for me it really helps to have
that physical activity between talking to
people (or instead of). I also recognise my
need for a lot of downtime after a show.*

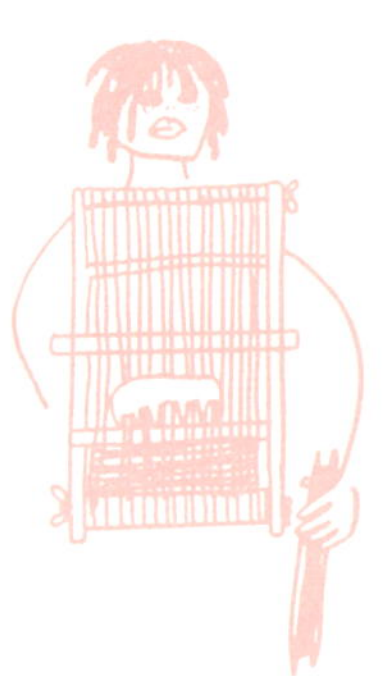

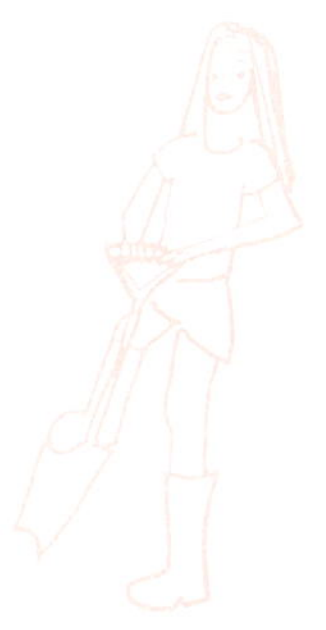

ASKING FOR WHAT YOU NEED

Many artists worry that being upfront about their needs and requirements will make them seem difficult and unprofessional. I believe the opposite to be true: explaining your circumstances clearly at the start of a working relationship is in fact highly professional. This might involve making an organisation aware of a health condition or disability, of your caregiving responsibilities or of a job that means you can't respond on certain days.

Artists with health issues or who are working with disabilities can write an access rider to share at the outset of a working relationship. This can include notification of mobility requirements, requests for extra time to respond to correspondence, details of their caregivers and so on. There are templates available online.

It is legitimate for any artist to establish boundaries to protect precious time in the studio or with their family. I find there are few things more freeing than setting an automatic email response during intense writing periods, releasing myself from the burden of politeness. You can also stipulate that people do not contact you about work after 5pm or over the weekend.

Establishing boundaries is not about refusing to participate, communicate or collaborate; it is about laying down the parameters within which this can happen.

If I am feeling overwhelmed by the amount of noise or number of people, I have found it useful to let people know that I need to take time for myself, exchange contact information if I want, and leave. That way, I have made a brief in-person connection and can follow up later by email.

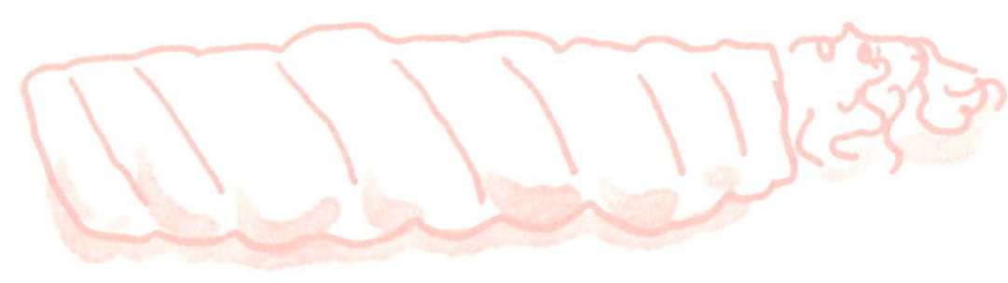

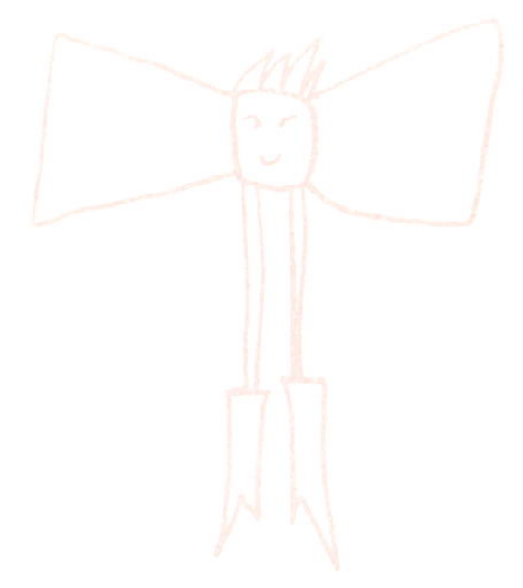

I limit the interactions I have and allow myself to prepare in advance, so that those I do have are more fruitful, and I'm not worn out by the time I get round to actually making my work. Virtual interviews and studio visits can be great since I can refer to notes more easily and avoid anxiety around eye contact. Whether virtual or in person, one-on-one interactions in quieter settings work much better for me, due to sensory and processing differences. I ask my partner and friends for support, either by being present or by talking through interactions. I have also worked with a mentor to help me navigate the bits I struggle with, and to grow in confidence.

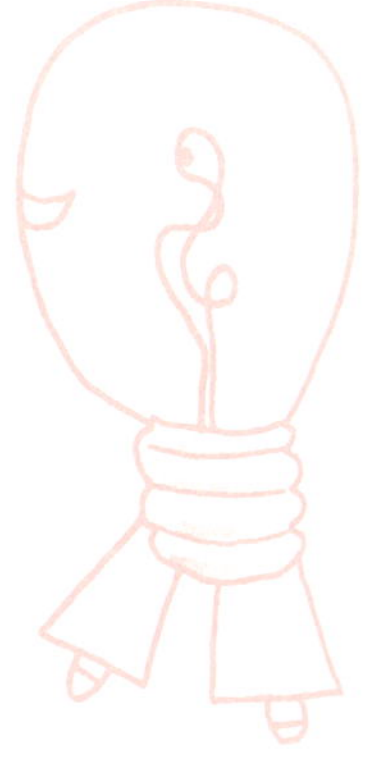

Daytime events feel less pressured than evenings. Having children there can feel like an icebreaker. One-on-one studio visits are good for being able to talk in depth. Whatever the nature of the event, I like to have a clear start time. If I'm visiting someone, I might do a recce first to get a feel of what the place is like. Hosting other artists to be part of my recent show took the pressure off me; I was able to join in and have fruitful discussions. Structured events are helpful. It is easier to attend when I know there is something to see/do at a certain time.

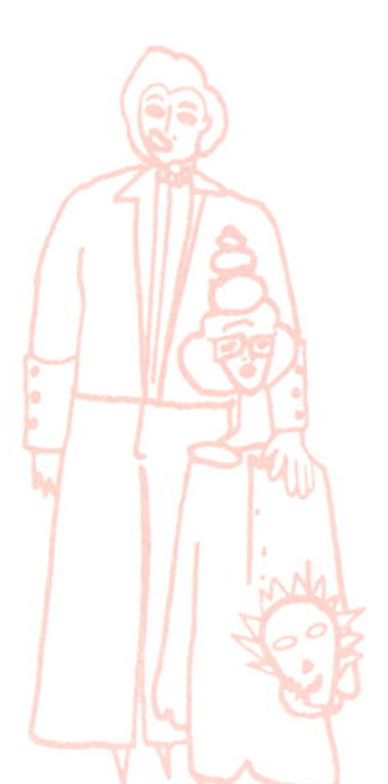

SPEAKING IN PUBLIC

I used to be terrified of public speaking. The cold sweats and shakes of the moment itself were preceded by days of anxiety and nights of insomnia. I remember having a book out about 15 years ago and thinking how ridiculous it was to be that scared of speaking about something on which I was literally a world expert. These days, a significant portion of my work comes from panel discussions, lectures, interviews, podcasts and radio broadcasts. It's been a long path to get here, and I'm afraid there's no easy, immediate, fix.

Unappealing as it is, the first thing to do is accept speaking opportunities and force yourself to get more used to them. Participating in panel discussions is much easier than speaking directly to an audience. You can (and should) focus completely on the person asking the questions, and on your fellow participants – part of your role on the panel is to support them too. Ahead of these events, I'd feel the butterflies mounting and would tell myself it was excitement. I'd even say it to people: 'I'm so excited about the talk this evening!' Ridiculous as this sounds, it helped take the edge off.

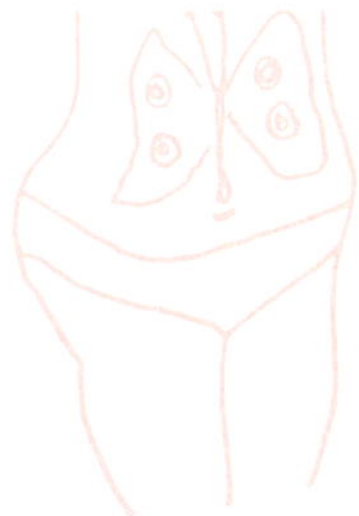

Once I became more comfortable with panel discussions, I started to go on small podcasts and local radio shows. I couldn't stand the sound of myself in the recordings. I remember going to a vocal coach and lamenting that I couldn't control my voice. He said that trying to control my voice was making me tense and was thus counterproductive. Instead, I should relax and slow down.

The real transformation came from doing improv

courses. Improvised comedy works on principles that are useful in all kinds of human interactions. The first is that you respond to anything said to you in the spirit of 'yes, and…'. In other words, you accept it and build on what has been offered to you rather than rejecting it or blocking it. The second is that everyone involved is there to support one another and move things forwards – this enterprise is bigger than you as an individual. In responding positively to and supporting other people, you learn to trust that they will support you in turn.

Speaking about your work as an artist is not like being a politician on the morning news. You are not auditioning for the role of prime minister. You don't need to know everything, be a world expert or even be slick. All people want is to hear a bit about your work and get a sense of who you are. When things go wrong – and they always will – it will be funny, human and relatable rather than a catastrophe.

Constantly force yourself to do really uncomfortable things – like speaking about your work in videos.

When it comes to public speaking, address one friendly-looking person in the crowd – this took a lot of practice.

I do like to put myself forward for things, but it is hard. When I did a talk recently for a Pecha Kucha night, I'd over-rehearsed my presentation, so I felt more comfortable.[24] The lights were low which was great for feeling more at ease. I also have a special stone which I can move between my fingers to ground me, and I used that throughout, rationalising to myself that if anyone noticed they'd just see it as an eccentric art thing rather than a weird thing.

SOCIAL MEDIA

The social media landscape changes rapidly. Over 20 years since the launch of Facebook and Myspace, platforms have soared and crashed, and the fortunes of artists whose careers were overly dependent on them have followed. Instagram has, in many ways, been tremendously empowering for artists, allowing them to disseminate images of their work and

---

24   Developed in Japan, Pecha Kucha is a presentation format for creative people – it offers each speaker a limited amount of time to share an ongoing project or recent work. In the classic Pecha Kucha format, each presentation features 20 slides displayed for 20 seconds each, meaning that every speaker gets 6 minutes and 40 seconds. Groups holding Pecha Kucha events can modify the format.

connect with peers, collectors and other arts professionals. It has been particularly valuable for those who, for whatever reason, are less able to be physically present at public events. It is also greedy for attention, can guzzle up your time and can encourage feelings of jealousy and inadequacy. It's a tricky balance to feel you are getting more out of social media than it gets out of you.

For a long time, the only way that I dealt with new people and situations was social media. It helped me build self-confidence and create a social bubble where I felt safe. It worked well in the beginning, but after years of existing that way as an artist, I felt that I had become stuck. The bubble was a trap, because the dissonance between my safe cave and the outer world became enormous.

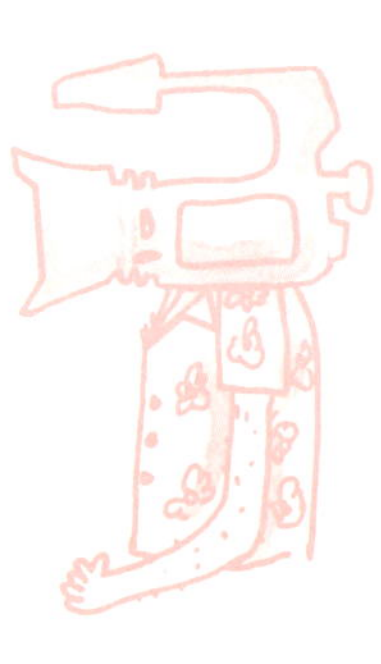

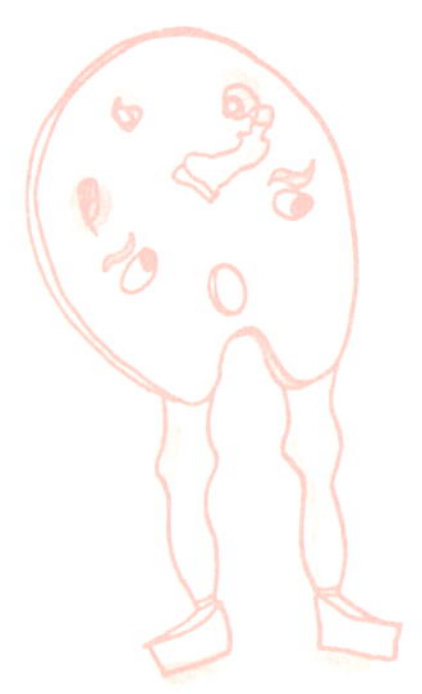

My main coping mechanism has been to try and step back from social media. As someone who works slowly with a lot of decision-making, I can get overwhelmed by all the art happening on Instagram. I've found reaching out to like-minded artists and connecting in small groups helps, rather than trying to be part of the larger 'noise'.

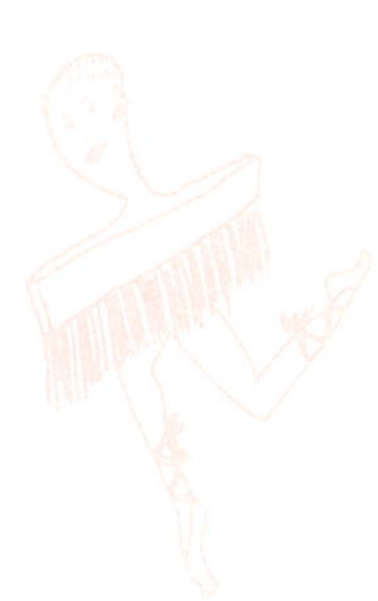

*Ahead of an event, connect with others
who will be present via social media. That
way you never walk into a room 'cold'.
Go to small events and events outside
of art capitals so folks start recognising
you when they see you in a big room.*

*I'm not sure how effective networking
is these days in terms of getting
your work out there. Historically,
I've got some projects from
networking, but these days it tends
to be more through social media
and then followed up with online
conversations and formal proposals.*

ON BALANCE

Art can be harsh. The work will refuse to resolve itself. People will say thoughtless things. You will get rejected. You will have exhibitions at which no works sell. There will be times when it seems all around you flourish while you flounder. You will feel too old, that your work is out of fashion, that you are too much or too little, the wrong this or wrong that.

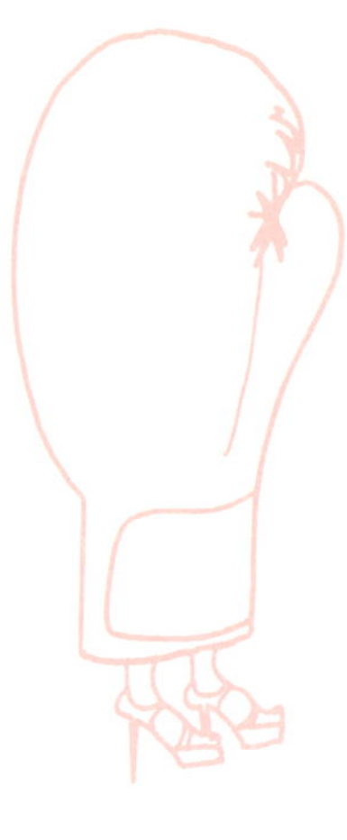

*Pick your battles and do what
feels enjoyable or necessary,
but never feel compelled.*

*Find something to boost your confidence
and apply non-stop for contests.*

*When I gather enough energy and
confidence to go out again, I will try my
best and it will take a few days to recover.
I am working on a few sentences that I
can have up my sleeve to ease my anxiety.*

*I work as an art psychotherapist for
teenagers with issues including crippling
anxiety. One strategy that I also use on
myself is to pretend to be the person
you'd wish to be. If I am struggling with
the confidence to approach someone,
or to keep pushing forward with my
work, I will imagine what a 'proper'
artist would do (in other words, a more
confident, successful one). It's a form of
faking it, but it translates into my work
through the construction of mythical
personalities. I have a character who
makes my work who is more confident
and accomplished than myself.*

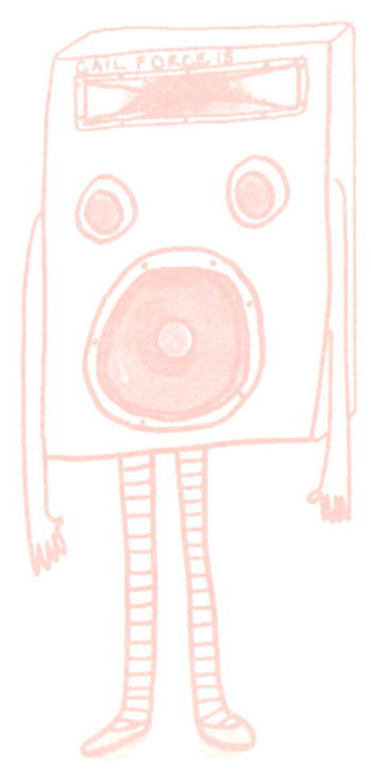

My main strategy has been to form close alliances with artists who 'get' me, and to nurture a microclimate of real acceptance. We frequently communicate and check in. We encourage action and we applaud each step forwards. I have also developed a toughness over the years, aligned with a sense of urgency. Being ill reminds me of the limited time we have, and to use it well. You cannot jump at the chance of an exhibition if you do not have a ready body of work that you are happy with.

As a child, I always felt I was on the outside looking in. This quality of observing things closely, being a watcher, made me a good artist.

I've always been very shy, but most would say the opposite about me. I try to put myself in new situations, talk about my work when inside I'm dying, keep saying yes to public visibility rather than running from it. I cover well. I haven't become less shy, but being in the world has become more familiar.

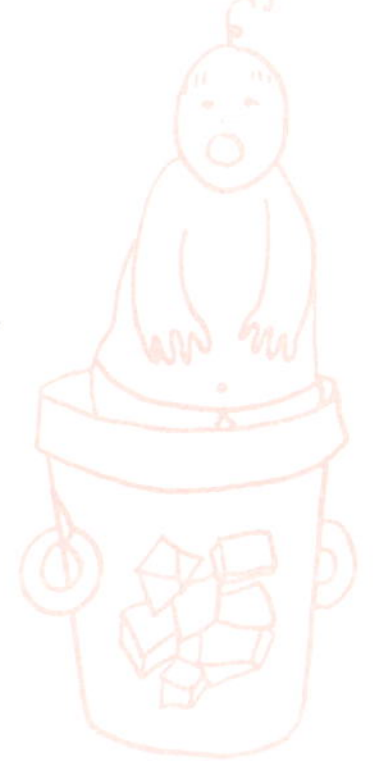

*I go into overwhelm very easily, so find
most interactions difficult. I'm able to hide
it mostly, but it does mean at networking
events I can present well but soon burn out
and have to make my excuses and leave. How
to cope? I try and ignore it but must admit
most days it knocks me hard. There's only
so much faking it to make it that I can do.*

*My coping mechanisms include
meditation, and growing confidence
that it's okay (more than okay!) to be
a quieter person. Trying to be someone
you're not only leads to more anxiety.*

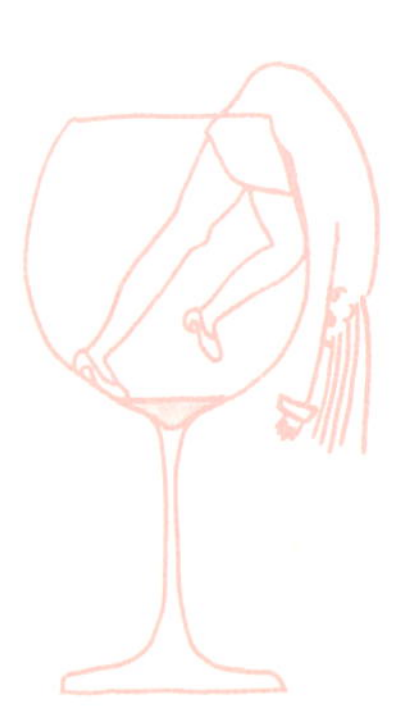

*I learned many tricks over the years
which basically boiled down to drinking
too much and playing a part. The better
that I got at it, the further away from
my work I became. I no longer have
coping strategies because the ones I
relied on are not good for my mental
health. Perhaps just be yourself and only
go to things if you genuinely want to –
not because you think you ought to?*

*I run my own space so we can make
our own non-neurotypical rules!*

If there's one goal I want you to take from this book, it's that of a sustainable career that will allow you to make art on your own terms for as long as you wish to. Achieving this will depend to varying degrees on economic factors, on being part of a supportive community and on your own self-belief. To add my voice to the Misfit Chorus one final time: it will also depend on your ability to maintain mental equilibrium in the face of events beyond your control.

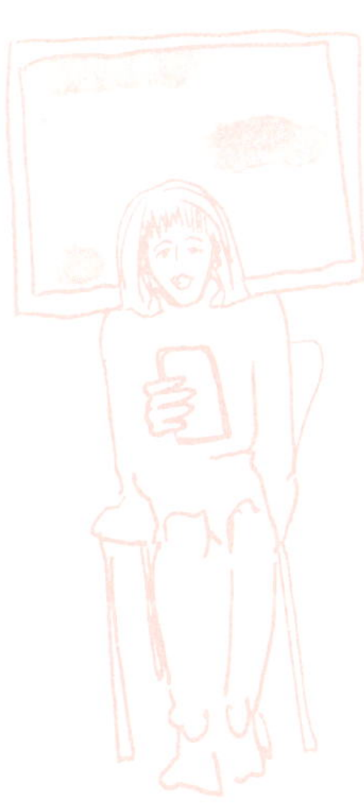

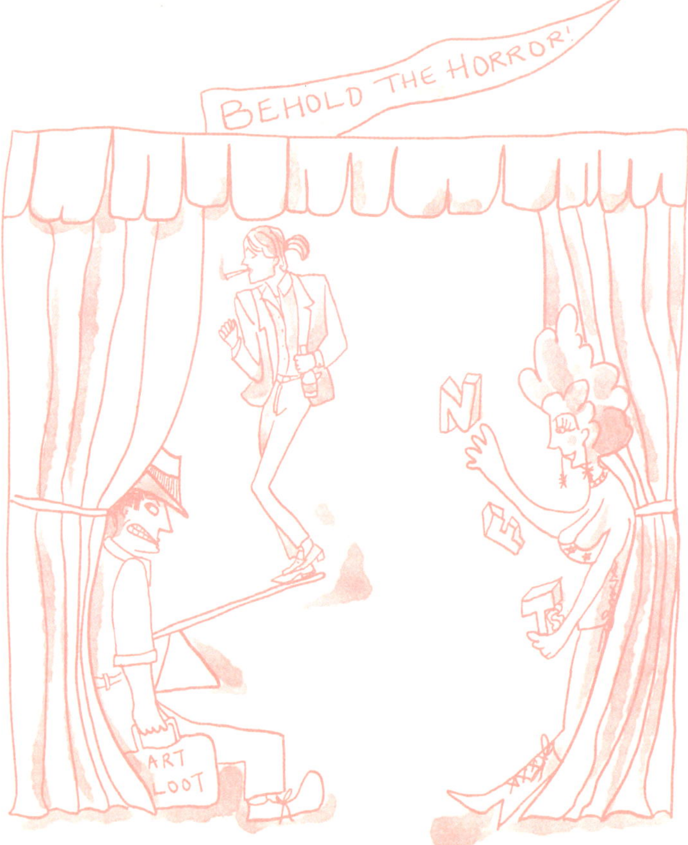

BEHOLD THE HORROR!
ART LOOT

THE HORROR SHOW

In putting together a grown-up guide to entering the art world, I have been forthright about its pitfalls and peculiarities. We've been around a bit, you and I, and we know that things don't always work out as expected – or as desired. Sometimes it's the result of plain bad luck. Sometimes you choose one route and for no predictable reason, the world chooses another one. Sometimes you make mistakes and need to accept them and move on. In our world, there are also many instances of exploitation, thoughtlessness and bad practice.

Despite artists being de facto the people with the least money in the art world, there is no shortage of schemes set up to exploit them. Part 10 looks at when things go wrong. Bad business models you want to avoid. Common art world scams. The pitfalls of social media. Avoiding painful social interactions, and what to do if you put your foot in it.

BAD BUSINESS

Artists get charged for many things, so judging when a fee is too high, or a situation exploitative, can be tricky. If you have committed to selling and promoting your own work, the cost of renting a gallery or showing in an art fair is a legitimate business expense so long as you are confident you can recoup it. Those self-same fees may seem shockingly high to an artist who isn't managing themself as a business. The question of when an expense is justified and when it is exploitative is not clear cut. Here are a few models I would be wary of.

Unpaid 'opportunities'. Our passion, hope, ambition and desire to be visible in a competitive environment make us vulnerable to unpaid demands on our time and labour. If you are asked to speak at an event or as part of a panel, you should be paid – both for the time it takes to prepare and the presentation itself. If you have to travel a considerable distance, you should also request transport costs. Artists from minority backgrounds should never be expected to speak unpaid for the sake of 'representation'.

It is standard to expect a fee for participation in a group show in a public gallery or institution, the exception being DIY shows in artist-run spaces. I believe artists should also be paid for group shows at commercial galleries. This is not currently the norm, but since it is notoriously difficult to sell work out of group shows, the artists are unlikely to make anything on sales. If you want to negotiate for a fee for participating in a group show at a commercial gallery, you could instead request an advance on sales of your work (i.e. if the gallery sells any of your work, they can recoup the fee out of that). It might not work, but it's important that we keep asking.

Feel free to remind anyone inviting you to participate in an event, or to lend or donate your artwork unpaid for the sake of 'exposure', that 'exposure' is not a currency recognised by supermarkets, utility companies or landlords, and that sadly you do require payment in the form of money to stay alive.

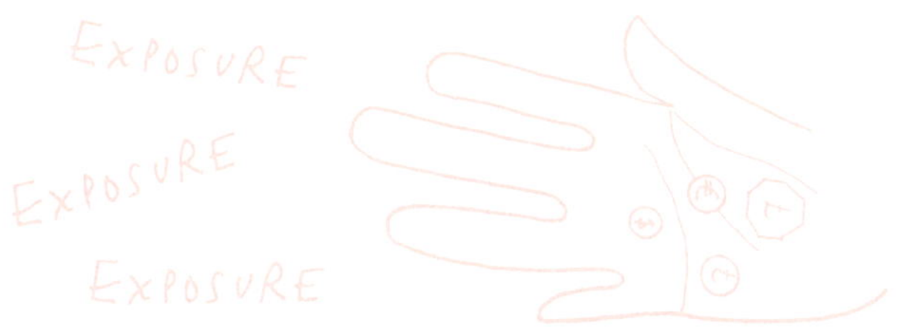

Residencies. It is common (though not universal) to charge a small application fee for artist residencies and to expect artists to pay for their own travel and some, or all, of their food. For me, there's a grey area around charging for accommodation. I know some grassroots residencies make accommodation available to artists at cost price or close to this – so there is a charge, but it's effectively subsidised. There are other residencies (often quite grand ones) which are pay-to-stay at levels comparable to a hotel. Granted, many extras may come as part of the package (studio access, a kiln, mentoring, networking...), but any 'residency' that is run on a for-profit model would more accurately be called a retreat. Nothing wrong with that, but let's be clear: this is a business, not a generous offer of support.

Galleries. Not all galleries represent artists – some are simply well-outfitted, white-walled rooms for hire. It's an old-fashioned model, one common in the 19th century, and one that has come back into vogue. Exhibition spaces for hire allow commercial galleries from other territories to test their artists in new markets – essentially they function like year-round art fairs. Many gallery complexes have spaces that are available on a short-term rental basis to artists and collectives as well as galleries.

For artists this can be confusing, particularly if you have been approached and offered the space for an exhibition, only to learn that you are expected to pay for it. I think it's iffy for galleries-for-hire to approach artists directly if they are going to charge them to exhibit. The artist often believes that they have been offered a show in a prestigious gallery; instead they're being invited to rent a space.[25] The result is often confusion, disappointment and a degree of hurt, as well as a large bill.

---

25 I assume galleries-for-hire approach artists because they want the exhibition programme to feel selective and curated.

If you receive an approach or are considering renting a gallery space for an exhibition, be clear on the terms. What do you get in return for the fee – will they send out invitations to their mailing list? Will they publicise your exhibition on social media? Will they help to install it? Will they provide an invigilator for the space while the show is on? Will they promote your work? Will they process sales? Do not be surprised if the answer to all of the above is no. You are essentially being offered terms applicable to a commercial gallery equipped with the personnel and infrastructure to do all this themselves. If the gallery is charging rent, they should not also expect commission on sales. It's an either/or situation. Any outfit looking to do both is taking the piss.

Oh, and while we're on the subject. Being invited to pay to participate in a group show is straightforwardly dodgy. Ok?

THE NFT AND OTHER SCAMS

The scenarios covered above may be exploitative, but they are perfectly legal. We are also in a golden era of scams, many of them taking advantage of our increasing reliance on technology for everything from banking to social interactions. If you receive any invitation, offer or commercial approach from an unfamiliar email address, phone number or social media account, be suspicious. If the offer sounds too good to be true, it almost certainly will be. As a basic precaution, copy and paste the email address, phone number or social media account handle into a search engine – if it comes from a real person or organisation, they should pop up immediately in the search and be contactable by other means. If not, it is likely to be a bot or scammer.

NFTs. For those lucky enough to have lived under a rock in 2021, or who need reminding, NFTs are digital artworks attached to blockchain – a.k.a. Non-Fungible Tokens. Think of them as the art equivalent of Bitcoin. NFTs have been around since the mid-2010s, but the term entered public consciousness in 2021 following market speculation that saw grotesque sums paid for unprepossessing digital art often made with the assistance of an AI. A rush of speculators started to generate NFTs in the hope of cashing in, but few (if any) made much from them. As is often the case in the art world, the big sales were divided among a handful of players. Nevertheless, NFTs now carry the association of big money.

If someone pops up in your social media comments or your direct messages, or sends you an email telling you they like your work and want to buy it or exhibit it as an NFT, delete the message, block the sender and report it – this is a scam. It reels you in through flattery – 'I love your artworks' – and the offer of a sales price in the thousands. It is you who will end up paying. Making an NFT version of your artwork (a.k.a. 'minting') will incur a fee. The scammer will either direct you to a doctored website set up to take your money and harvest your data, or they will offer to take care of the minting process themselves if you, ahem, forward them money for the fee.

Golden opportunity. The golden opportunity scam targets artists through emails and WhatsApp messages purportedly from well-known art world figures (Jerry Saltz and Damien Hirst are popular choices) or a famous commercial gallery. Care has often been taken over the design of these messages, and they may carry a plausible corporate logo (let down, often, by iffy spelling and grammar). They will offer lavish praise and explain that the author is working on a group show and would like to feature your work. If you respond positively, you will be told that there is an upfront fee for participating in this prestigious event. In reality, the show does not exist, your money will disappear and the message will certainly not have been from its supposed author.

Lovely offers and surprises do happen in the art world. It may have been that you once drove a truck alongside Jerry Saltz or went to primary school with Damien Hirst or dog-sat for the senior director of Lisson Gallery. If you are wavering over the possibility that this golden opportunity might be real, first check the email address by pasting it into a search engine – if it's attached to a real person they will appear in the search. Second, try calling them on the phone – at a registered office number – asking for confirmation. It may be that their account was hacked. In the astonishingly unlikely (sorry) scenario where the person named on the letter answers or returns your call through their official number and confirms that they are indeed offering you a golden opportunity – congratulations!

Again – being invited to pay to participate in a group show is straightforwardly dodgy.

Money transfers. There have been some shocking scams targeting smaller galleries, with criminals hacking into email accounts and sending counterfeit messages redirecting collectors to pay into their accounts rather than the gallery's. For this reason, many galleries now have security precautions around payments. This can be as simple as setting up a phone or video call and asking for verbal confirmation of bank details. I would suggest that you do likewise, particularly for sales made online to people you don't know.

There are other common scams to look out for. In one, a purchaser claims to have accidentally overpaid you, sends a screenshot of the transfer and asks to be reimbursed the excess amount. The original payment won't have been completed, so you'll end up transferring this 'overpayment' to a scammer. You may also be approached by people who ask you to ship a work as a gift for a spouse who is (naturally) a fan. They don't want to 'spoil the surprise' by making a payment out of their joint account, so will ask you to send the work on the understanding that payment will be made on receipt. It will not.

Paid content. The approach for a paid content scam will usually be made through direct messages on social media. Someone purporting to be from a magazine, blog or popular account will 'reach out', praise your work and offer you coverage. They'll describe the vast audience your work will reach if featured on their platform (the account contacting you may well have an impressive number of followers, which are likely paid-for). The catch: to be featured, you'll need to pay a fee.

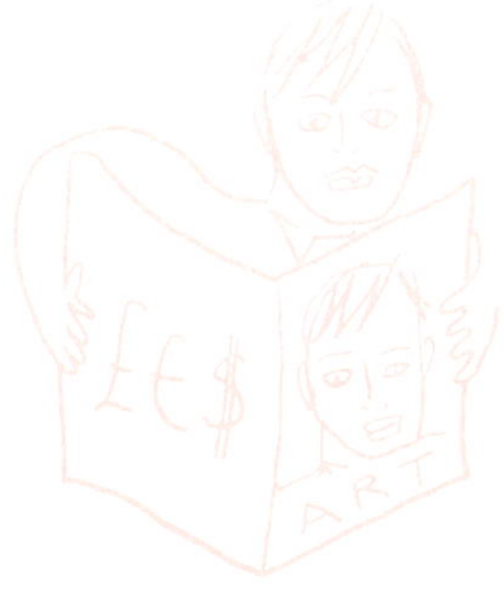

Having worked since the 1990s in art media, please believe me that this is not how getting magazine coverage works. Artists receive coverage in art publications because a) they have a major exhibition opening in the territory covered by that publication, b) the journalist and/or editor is excited by their work or c) their work feels in some way emblematic of that moment, and thus worthy of comment. If a journalist on a reputable publication (or blog, or podcast) wishes to interview you, they may make a first approach over social media, but there will not be a fee involved – if anything, it is they who should buy you a cup of coffee, rather than vice versa.

As with many art-world-related scams, the paid-content scam is compelling because it hovers close to questionable but legal practice. Competition for coverage in the art media is not a level field. There are advertisers who may anticipate coverage of their gallery's exhibitions as part of their deal with a magazine; powerful PR agencies skilled in grabbing editors' and journalists' attention; journalists who are taken on expenses-paid press trips to events such as the Venice Biennale in return for coverage of a specific pavilion or exhibition; and content sponsored by advertisers – a.k.a. 'sponcon' – which closely resembles commissioned articles. Arguably, much of this is – or comes very close to – paid content, but those doing the paying will almost always be organisations (galleries, museums, national pavilions) rather than individual artists. In general, the art media prides itself on its independence and resistance to hype and bribery.

The bottom line: if you are approached and offered paid-for content, delete the message and block the account.

SOCIAL MEDIA TRANSGRESSIONS

Beyond the realms of bots, scammers and bad actors, social media can be an important platform for artists.

If social media depresses you and makes you feel less fabulous than your peers, remember that you are basing this impression on highly edited fragments of their lives. Most are keener to share successes than failures – the prizes, grants and opportunities we have been awarded, the exhibitions we have helped organise, our trip to a special museum. Not visible are years of rejections, the baby keeping you awake all night or the cat sick you cleared up before your first cup of tea.

Even some decades in, the etiquette of these virtual spaces can be tricky. What constitutes a meaningful interaction with someone, sufficient – for example – to send a message letting them know about an upcoming exhibition, or inviting them for a studio visit? One 'like'? Absolutely not. A follow? Not quite yet. A follower who comments positively and meaningfully on a post? That's more like it.

It perhaps goes without saying that you should behave towards others online as you would hope for people to behave to you or someone you care about. People with large followings are still people. Even very positive messaging can feel 'off'. There are levels of engagement that feel obsessive to those on the receiving end – highly personal responses to everything someone posts, barrages of unsolicited messages, a tone of discourse that would suggest the target of this attention is a personal friend rather than someone encountered over social media.

Feeling that you know people you follow online is a form of parasocial relationship – the one-sided bond we can form with celebrities. (I once had an intense conversation with the actress Daniela Nardini at the Roots & Fruits grocery in Glasgow, convinced that she was a friend whose name escaped me.) Because we can see them cold-water swimming and walking their dog, social media presents a convincing illusion of a meaningful two-way relationship with people in the public eye. It may not feel that way to the person you are following, who finds themself on the receiving end of too much online attention from a person they have never met.

Trickiest to navigate is that zone where social media relationships cross into the physical world. Friendships and professional relationships formed online can become friendships and professional relationships offline, but agreeing to meet a fellow artist for a coffee is one thing, spotting someone prominent you follow online IRL is another. Don't assume that they will know who you are, even if you've exchanged messages. Don't write them off as an arsehole just because they don't recognise you.

By all means introduce yourself. State your name clearly, tell them that you are an artist and explain that you follow them on social media. Say something short and positive about their work ('I really enjoyed your last show'). If they seem amenable, follow that up with a quick professional question ('What are you working on at the moment?'). Then remove yourself from the interaction ('Lovely to meet you in real life, enjoy the evening!'). If you meet them again on another occasion, please introduce yourself by name and contextualise yourself again. And again. And again. Each time. As someone who constantly forgets names, I find

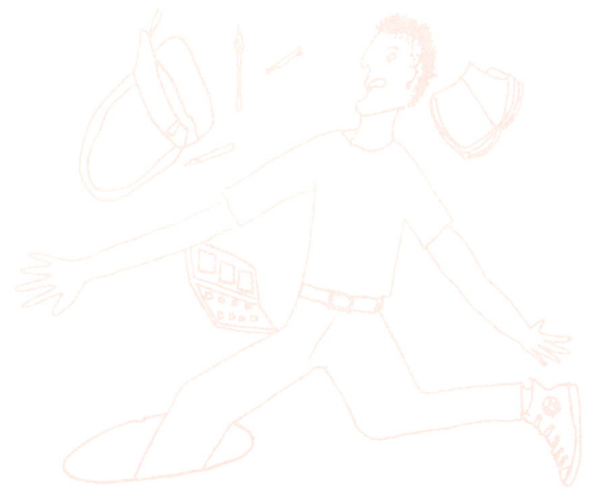

having people reintroducing themselves an incredible kind-
ness. Not only am I spared the embarrassment of admitting
I've forgot, but I get to pretend that I'm much less of an idiot
than I really am by then pretending that I remembered.

ON MESSING UP

It takes oomph and gumption just to keep going in the art
world, let alone to succeed on your chosen path. I have
instructed you to be bold and fearless. It also behoves me

to note that you can push such things too far. In Part 5, I introduced Lady Kitt's idea of the 'wanker tipping point' as a metric for entitled behaviour (p.71). How do you guard against tipping into wankerdom? If you enter the wanker-sphere, is there a route back out?

Like all people, artists can, and often do, pass the tipping point. They may not be sensitive to circumstances. For example, they might be determined to promote their own work to gallerists at an art fair or private view (see Part 7 for a refresher on why this is a bad idea, p.117). They may also not be sensitive to how they come across. The tone they adopt to appear strong and self-confident might instead seem confrontational, intimidating and even aggressive. This is a particular risk if you are an older person speaking to a younger person, more so if you are an older man speaking to a younger woman. Our perception of another person's high status within the art world may well not accord with theirs – or indeed their sense of personal vulnerability.

Messing up in the art world is more often the result of low-level entitlement and solipsism than spectacular fall-outs and cock-ups. If I make a mental note not to work with someone again, it will be because they have been thought-less, high-handed, selfish or rude.

That being said, we all have off days. If you feel you have not behaved as you would have wished, send an immediate apology (an actual apology, featuring the word 'sorry', not a series of excuses or justifications). The mes-sage should be short, just a sentence or two. If the recipient emails or messages you back, all is ok. If they do not, then you have upset them, and that working relationship is probably blown – at least for the time being. Do not send further emails following up. It is for them to get in touch if/when they are ready.

Some artists' tactics to get their work seen can be read as pushiness, harassment and even bullying by those on the receiving end. This can go as far as cascades of passive-aggressive emails, or unannounced visits to a gallery, studio or home address. No one should feel coerced, emotionally blackmailed or forced to look at your work. Even leaving aside the interpersonal unpleasantness, it won't do you any favours for someone to engage with it under duress – there should never be a question of getting your work seen 'at any cost'.

There is a particular genre of artist that considers being contrary and high-handed an important part of their 'persona'. I imagine they see themselves building on the legacy of modernist provocateurs like artist, poet and pugilist Arthur Cravan (the goals of whose very short life were to get noticed and piss people off). It may be diverting to scandalise the art world for a few years, and it can certainly be fun to watch from a distance, but as a career strategy, 'hellraiser' lacks longevity. By all means go for it if you care not a fig for friends, collectors, gallerists or institutional relationships.

A caveat: most of the time when you think you have said or done something terrible, the other party is entirely oblivious. Particularly at events that make us anxious (such as private views), we get our brains and our words tangled. In art as in romance, this happens precisely when you encounter someone you've longed to talk to but don't know well. You may leave the interaction and the event feeling that you've said something weird, ill-judged or offensive. The likelihood is that the person in question didn't even notice, has forgotten it already or (at worst) found the interaction mildly awkward in the moment but thought little of it. You will lie awake all night freaking out about it. They will not.

Even many senior people in the art world are socially awkward. This includes the directors of commercial galleries and public institutions. Critics and journalists are even worse. We work in a sector populated by perpetual square pegs. Many of us compound our awkwardness by spending great stretches of our working lives on our own, kept company by our wayward thoughts. As a result, we often rub one another up the wrong way, misread situations, succumb to jealousy, resentment and self-pity, say stupid things, get offended and fall out. Add to the mix the fact that much art world interaction happens in a strange social hinterland between the professional and the personal. And often involves alcohol. It's a potent formula for explosive interactions. If you can, be kind, generous-spirited and forgiving. Failing that, do try not to be a total wanker.

RESOURCES

Please visit the online Resources page for links to artists' associations, unions, networks and support groups, alternative art schools, short courses and correspondence courses and other organisations that might be useful as you (re)enter the art world.

hoxtonminipress.com/pages/art-world-resources

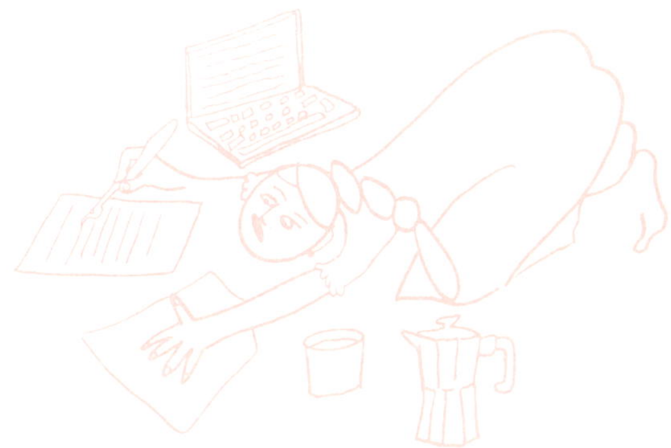

HETTIE JUDAH

Hettie Judah is a writer and curator. Art critic for
The i Paper between 2016 and 2024, she is a regular
contributor to *The Guardian*, *The Times Literary
Supplement*, *Apollo* and *Frieze*. Curator of the acclaimed
exhibition *Acts of Creation: On Art and Motherhood*, she
has authored numerous books on art and is well known as
a broadcaster and advocate for artists' rights.

JEMIMA BURRILL

Jemima Burrill is an artist, curator, filmmaker,
photographer and gardener. She draws daily and is
motivated by how creativity supports wellbeing. Her
work has been shown internationally, and her practice
includes facilitating talks, salons and shared spaces for
creative exchange.

HOXTON MINI PRESS

Hoxton Mini Press is a small indie publisher based in
east London. We are committed to making beautiful but
affordable books that don't screw up the planet. We offset
all our printing, and we hope that the trees we do use
will continue their life as books that you'll pass on to
your grandchildren.

WITH THANKS TO

All who came to TJ Boulting in September 2022 for the conversations that provided the foundation for this book, among them Ingrid Berthon-Moine, Emma Franks, Elsa James, Permindar Kaur, Paula MacArthur, Barry Sykes, Ehryn Torrell and Samar F. Zia, and Hannah Watson for hosting us.

All who responded to my questions with such enthusiasm, in particular the 'Misfit Chorus': Marzena Ablewska-Lech, Michele Allen, Iain Andrews, Betsy Bradley, Tereza Bušková, Lucy Churchill, Jo Cope, Andy Cropper, Jemma Cullen, Frances Earnshaw, Liz Elton, Camille Eskell, Rachel Fallon, Francesca Ferreri, Briana Frederick, Jez Riley French, Louise Halpern, Makiko Harris, Geraldine Hudson, Helen Kaplinsky, Stephanie Lamprea, Michele Landel, Lior Locher, Ellen Starr Lyon, Bobby Madrigal, Joanne Masding, Caroline McAuliffe, Claire Morgan, Bakula Nayak, Callum O'Reilly, Ruth Parker, Jaime Maria Pia, Emma Plunkett, Simona Ruscheva, Joanna Selick, Sellvida, Carrie Stanley, Jennie Syson, Nele Tas and others who prefer to remain anonymous.

Lady Kitt for providing the 'wanker tipping point', which became a central idea for the book – and its final word.

Anonymous gallerists in various territories for trusting me with their (at times shockingly) frank insights.

My agent Emma Smith for finding the book a perfect home with Hoxton Mini Press – who in turn provided a perfect editor in the great Flo Ward. Thanks to Martin, Ann and all at HMP for having faith, and Dom for making this book beautiful.

Jemima for her gorgeous, funny, heartfelt illustrations.

Ben for his support, patience, frank feedback, and pre-eminence as a Doggy Doppelganger.